S0-BZN-079

Contents

vii   **Connecting with Your PowerBook** • • • • • • • • • • **introduction**

xi   Darling, you look marvelous!
xvii   A few keyboard highlights
xxi   Rest stop

1   **The Care and Feeding of Your PowerBook** • • • • • • • • **chapter 1**

3   Cases
7   Keyboard and screen protectors
9   Cleaning inside and out
10   Rest stop

11   **The Start of a Beautiful Friendship** • • • • • • • • • • • • **chapter 2**

13   System Preferences that matter
29   Cruising the Internet superhighway
40   Ah, that wonderful feeling of control

41   **Organize Your Life** • **chapter 3**

43   Manage contacts with Address Book
47   The right place at the right time with iCal
53   Random notes with Stickies
56   That great feeling of organization

PowerBook
Fan Book

57   **Refine Your Digital Lifestyle** • • • • • • • • • • • • • • • • **chapter 4**

59   Get the picture with iPhoto
67   The joy of digital music
76   Transform dull video into exciting iMovies
83   Are you feeling digital?

85   **PowerBook on the Go** • **chapter 5**

87   Between you and your PowerBook
89   Uniquely USB
92   Wireless wonders
95   Extend your PowerBook's memory
97   And for the serious road warrior . . .
99   Final stop

100   **Index** •

Introduction: Connecting with Your PowerBook

Connecting with Your PowerBook

Care and Feeding

Getting Started

Organize Your Life

Your Digital Lifestyle

PowerBook on the Go

Your PowerBook represents the pinnacle of Apple engineering. It has evolved over the years to become the finest laptop available anywhere, on any platform.

On the outside, Apple shunned the common black plastic that previously dominated laptop design and replaced it with a brushed aluminum alloy enclosure. Release the latch and press the power button, and you're greeted with Mac OS X—a modern, innovative operating system. Plus, the PowerBook comes loaded with all the productivity software you need to manage everything from your appointment calendar to your digital photo library. This explains some of the PowerBook's appeal.

But there's another tantalizing trait that's seldom covered in magazine articles or online reviews. It's the PowerBook's ability to bond with its owner. For many folks, the PowerBook becomes an extension of their own thinking, helping them to remember important information, organize their work, and even manifest their creative vision.

The process of building this friendship and making Apple's PowerBook *your PowerBook* is a rewarding one, as long as you have some idea about how to proceed. Many computer books attempt to tell you everything there is to know about that complicated machine staring back at you from the table. This overwhelms most people, and they end up closing the book, turning off the computer, and engaging in some other activity that's less intimidating. In so doing, they're simply accepting the status quo and never really making the computer their own. Ironically, the manual they bought to help them master the computer becomes as mysterious and challenging as the device itself.

That won't happen here.

What I've discovered during my years of helping people switch to the Mac, is that more often than not, they don't want to learn every intimate detail about their computer. After all, when you first strike up a friendship with somebody, do you really want to know every aspect of his life? Sometimes a little mystery is a good thing.

The Apple 15" PowerBook G4.

Connecting with Your PowerBook

Care and Feeding

Getting Started

Organize Your Life

Your Digital Lifestyle

PowerBook on the Go

Instead, most new Mac users just want to *feel comfortable* with their purchase. They want to learn the helpful and cool stuff right away while leaving the innermost technical details to the geeks who appreciate that level of complexity.

If your goal is to become friends with your PowerBook, this guide is for you. I spend the precious time I have with you *focusing on the things that you need to know* so you can bond quickly with this wonderful machine. I introduce you to lots of great accessories that extend the PowerBook's functionality, while ensuring that it remains as beautiful to admire as it was the first day you brought it home.

As you become comfortable with this computer, you may want to learn more about a specific area, such as using your PowerBook for video editing. I include links to informative web sites and helpful books that delve deeply into those specific functions.

First, let's all get to know each other. I'll start with explaining the various ports and buttons positioned all around the PowerBook's exterior. We'll take a few minutes to learn about cases and cleaners that will protect your investment and maintain that gorgeous metallic sheen. Then I'll introduce you to the important System Preferences that enable you to customize the PowerBook's behavior and appearance. That will lead us forward to an exploration of some of the great software that can make your life more organized, productive, and creative.

The final stage of bonding focuses on one of my favorite aspects of technology: toys. Yes, I have lots of enticing stuff that not only extends the functionality of your PowerBook, but is also truly fun to play with. So if you're reading about System Preferences and see an illustration for a wireless mouse, you'll know that I'm just providing you with a little toy relief. I'll show you how to accessorize your Mac to ensure that you have the coolest computer on the block.

We call this guide the *PowerBook Fan Book* because there is something different about PowerBook owners. For us, it's not just a computer. It's a device that we like and enjoy spending time with. We're fans, not just owners. And as far as I'm concerned, there's nothing wrong with having an appreciation for the tools that add richness to our lives.

Darling, you look marvelous!

The PowerBook comes in three sizes: 12," 15," and 17". And they are gorgeous. The size refers to the diagonal measurement of the screen, not the outside dimensions. The 12" PowerBook for example, actually measures 10.9" by 8.6" on the outside. The 15" model weighs in at 13.7" by 9.5" And the granddaddy of them all, the 17" PowerBook, is a whopping 15.4" by 10.2". This is handy to know when you start thinking about cases and other accessories. But no matter how you measure it, the PowerBook packs a lot of computer in to a very svelte package.

It's also amazing how little so much power weighs. These laptops tip the scale at 4.6, 5.7, and 6.9 pounds respectively. In metric, that's 2.1, 2.6, and 3.1 kilograms. When you realize that one of these machines can replace an entire desktop system, the weight-to-performance ratio is incredible.

Much in the same way that you'd walk around a new car and kick its tires, I want to show you some of the PowerBook's external features.

For starters, here's how you open it.

Press the oblong-shaped metal button on the front edge of the computer and the lip pops open part way. Put your thumb underneath the middle of the lip of the lid, and gently push upward. The hinge is usually a little stiff, so you might want to hold the base of the computer with your other hand while doing so. Adjust the screen so it's at a comfortable viewing angle.

The PowerBook lets you know it's sleeping with the pulsing light on the left side of the cover latch.

Connecting with Your PowerBook

Care and Feeding

Getting Started

Organize Your Life

Your Digital Lifestyle

PowerBook on the Go

By the way, when you opened the lid you may have noticed a short gray plastic strip along each upper edge. That is where Apple has stashed the AirPort and Bluetooth antenna. So when you open the lid, you're actually raising the antenna.

With the lid open, you'll see the power button above the keyboard to the right of the hinge. Press it once and your PowerBook will begin the start-up process. In computer terms, this is called *booting the system*. After a couple minutes, you're ready to log in and begin working.

But before doing so, I have a few tips for you. First, you can put your PowerBook to sleep by holding down the power button for a second or two. You'll be greeted with a dialog box presenting you with four options: Restart, Sleep, Cancel, or Shut Down. Sleep darkens the screen and idles the processor. This conserves precious battery life when you're not using the PowerBook, and saves you from having to reboot completely. To wake up the PowerBook, hit any key, and it springs back to life.

Hard Shut Down in Emergency

Mac OS X is one of the most stable operating systems available today, but that doesn't mean that it's infallible. You can crash the OS and freeze your PowerBook. If that happens, hold down the power button for a few seconds to shut down your computer. After it has come to a complete rest, press the power button again to reboot. By the same token, when you want to put your Mac to sleep via the power button, only hold it down for about a second. You'll immediately be greeted with a dialog box presenting you with the sleep option.

You can also put it to sleep by closing the lid until it latches. You'll know that the PowerBook is actually asleep because a light next to the oblong latch button will pulse gently, like a heartbeat. To awaken the PowerBook, push the latch button and pop open the lid. It comes back to life!

The general rule of thumb is that you can let the PowerBook sleep when not in use for 24 hours or less when it's running off its battery. (Plugged into the wall, it makes no difference.) Longer than that and you might want to shut it down completely so there isn't any battery drain over extended periods of time. Eventually, if left in sleep mode and running off the battery, your PowerBook will shut down altogether.

PowerBooks also provide for lid-closed operation with an external monitor. After your display is connected, put the PowerBook to sleep by closing its lid. Then activate it by pressing a key on an external keyboard. (Yes, you need an external keyboard for this trick or typing will be really difficult.) The PowerBook will then dedicate all of its video memory to the external monitor.

Note however, you don't have to close your PowerBook to send the video signal to an external monitor. If you leave the lid up, you can choose between mirroring and spanning. *Mirroring,* as you might guess, presents the same information on both the external monitor and your PowerBook's LCD. *Spanning,* on the other hand, expands your visual real estate by enabling you to show different items on the two screens. This is really helpful when you have applications with lots of pallets, such as Photoshop. You can use the external monitor as your main work area and the PowerBook's LCD as the home for pallets and other tools.

Now take a look at the front edge of the PowerBook (15" and 17"). To the right of the latch you'll see the opening for the slot-loading optical drive. This is where you insert CDs and DVDs. To eject them, press the Eject button—it looks a lot like something you'd find on your VCR—in the far upper-right of the keyboard. On the 12" model the optical drive is located on the right side of the computer, but works in just the same way.

Apple refers to its two types of optical drives as the Combo and the SuperDrive. The Combo can read and write to compact discs (CD-R and CD-RW), as well as read DVDs. The SuperDrive adds the ability to write to DVD-R discs as well.

There's a lot more happening on the left side. The 12" models have all of their ports here, while the 15" and 17" PowerBooks spread their ports out on both sides of the computer. How about a quick port tour?

Connecting with
Your PowerBook

Care and
Feeding

Getting
Started

Organize
Your Life

Your Digital
Lifestyle

PowerBook on
the Go

The left side of the PowerBook features ports for AC power, modem, USB, line-in, and headphones, and the PC card slot.

Starting from the back on the left side is the AC power jack. Here's where you connect the external power adapter to charge the battery and run the laptop. Next is the modem port (RJ-11). A cable is included with your accessories, and you can use it to connect the built-in 56K V.92 modem to your average phone jack for dial-up Internet service.

On the 15" and 17" PowerBooks, you have one of two USB 2.0 ports on the left side (there's another on the right) that enables you to download information from a variety of devices including most digital cameras and memory card readers. Also, if you want to use a mouse instead of the PowerBook's built-in trackpad, this is where you'd connect it. I appreciate the Apple engineers who put USB ports on both sides of the computer (15" and 17" only). In everyday use this is a noticeable convenience. You should also note that USB 2.0 is backwards compatible with USB 1.1. This means that chances are good that your older USB devices will work with your new PowerBook.

The compact 12" PowerBooks aligns all of its ports on the left side of the computer.

The 12" PowerBook puts a 10/100 Ethernet jack (RJ-45) next to the modem port. Primary uses for this port include connecting to cable and DSL modems and company networks. The 15" and 17" models put this port on the left side and have expanded its capability to 10/100/1000 Ethernet, also referred to as Gigabit Ethernet.

The next port on the 12" PowerBook is for FireWire 400. The most common use is for connecting your iPod or external hard drive. The 15" and 17" models place this port on the right side next to the other USB 2.0 connector.

The 12" model also has a mini-DVI jack on this side. Digital Video (DV) output provides a pure digital connection from the PowerBook's graphics card to the DVI-equipped display for outstanding image quality. The 12" model comes with an adapter to connect from this mini port to a DVI display. The 15" and 17" models feature a full-sized DVI port on the left side.

All three models put two stereo mini jacks near the front on the left side. The one further back is "line-in" and the one closer to the front is for output to headphones and external speakers. Often folks are disappointed that they can't connect a regular microphone to the line-in port and record. It won't work because line-in is for amplified sources such as from your stereo. You'll be happy to know, however, that your PowerBook has a built-in omnidirectional microphone that works extremely well. Where is it? Apple has cleverly hidden it in the left speaker grille on the 15" and 17" models, and in the upper-left corner, above the keyboard, on the 12" version—see that little pinhole just above the F1 key?

Now we get to one of my favorite PowerBook features (on the 15" and 17" models only)—the PC card expansion slot that accepts one Type I or Type II card. In everyday use, I have an adapter that enables me to insert the memory cards from my digital camera directly into the

PC Card adapters, such as this model from SanDisk, enable you to insert your digital camera memory directly into your 15" or 17" PowerBook (*www.sandisk.com* about $10, memory cards not included.)

Connecting with
Your PowerBook

Care and
Feeding

Getting
Started

Organize
Your Life

Your Digital
Lifestyle

PowerBook on
the Go

PowerBook. This is a wonderful convenience because PC card adapters take up much less room in my case than dedicated memory card readers. But I can also use this slot to expand the PowerBook in many ways, including adding additional USB or FireWire ports if needed.

So far there's one more item on the left side that we haven't accounted for yet (on the 12" and 17" models)—the security slot. To make sure no one walks off with your computer when you're not there, attach a security cable here and lock it to your desk. You can find this slot on the right side of the 15" model.

The 15" PowerBook puts 6 ports on the right side too, including DVI, S-Video, Gigabit Ethernet, FireWire 800, FireWire 400, and USB 2.0.

You have two more ports to explore on the right side of the 15" and 17" models—FireWire 800 and S-Video. FireWire 800 is literally twice as fast as 400 (800 Mbps versus 400 Mbps) and sports a different type of connector. But most people use it for connecting to the latest (and fastest) model external hard drives, just as with FireWire 400.

S-Video is handy for connecting your PowerBook (15" and 17" models) to televisions, VCRs, and other video equipment. You can connect S-Video to S-Video, or use the S-Video-to-composite adapter (RCA male jack) that's included with your PowerBook. This comes in very handy if you want to use your laptop as an emergency DVD player with a television on the road or at a friend's house.

A few keyboard highlights

Let's take a look at the keyboard for a moment. It looks much like most other keyboards you've been using for years, except there are a few special keys worth mentioning (and the keyboard itself is probably more handsome than what you're accustomed to).

The F1 and F2 keys control screen brightness. Sure you could open the Displays system preference pane to adjust the brightness, but why go to that hassle when you can dim (F1) and brighten (F2) directly from the keyboard?

F3 allows you to mute all computer sounds. This might be a good control to use when checking email or instant messaging during an important meeting in the CEO's office. After all, you want her to think you're concentrating on her comments and not glancing at email from your best friend. F4 and F5 are for decreasing and increasing the volume. These are helpful when you're listening to music or watching a movie and want to make a quick adjustment.

The standard keyboard layout will seem familiar, but there are some convenient controls here too.

Introduction

Connecting with
Your PowerBook

Care and
Feeding

Getting
Started

Organize
Your Life

Your Digital
Lifestyle

PowerBook on
the Go

Avoid Embarrassing Start Ups!

A good rule of thumb is to keep the volume set low on your PowerBook. This is particularly important when starting the computer in quiet environments. It will "remember" the prior volume setting, and sound the start up chimes at that same level when booting. I learned this lesson the hard way once when I launched my PowerBook during a tense moment in a crowded courtroom. Suddenly all eyes were on me.

F6 is the number lock toggle button. When you activate *num lock,* you transform your typing keyboard into a calculator keypad. The letter *J* for example, becomes the number 1 when using Apple's Calculator application.

F7 toggles video mirroring on and off. This is particularly handy when you've connected your PowerBook to a projector and want to see the same thing on your monitor as is being projected on the big screen. When mirroring is off, you're in spanning mode, which can be quite disorienting, especially when speaking before a large audience.

On the 15" and 17" models, F8–F10 control the illuminated, fiber-optic backlit keyboard. F8 turns off the backlighting, F9 dims it, and F10 increases its brightness. Speaking of the illuminated keyboard, the PowerBook has light sensors that will automatically activate the keyboard backlighting in dimly lit environments. The sensors are beneath the speaker grille. You can activate this function in the Keyboard & Mouse preference pane (see Chapter 2 for more information on System Preferences.) On the 12" PowerBook, these three keys are open to custom programming.

Function keys F11 and F12 can be programmed for everyday tasks on all models, such as saving a document. Open System Preferences (Apple icon on the *Menu Bar → System Preferences*), then click on the Keyboard & Mouse icon. Now click on the Keyboard Shortcuts button within the preference pane. Click on the "+" button on the left side of the pane, and you'll be able to configure a function key.

PowerBook
Fan Book

The 15" and 17" models offer fiber-optic backlit keyboards.

To test this on your 12" PowerBook, type "Save" in the Menu Title field, and then hit the Tab key to move you to the Keyboard Shortcut field. Now press the F8 button. You have just programmed that button to save a document while working in any application.

Another group of keys that I think are real timesavers are the arrow keys on the lower-right corner of the keyboard. I think they are most useful when scrolling up and down long pages, such as when viewing Web pages in Safari. Try using the up and down arrows next time you're browsing the Web. I think you'll find the arrow keys easier to use than the trackpad.

Care and
Feeding

Getting
Started

Organize
Your Life

Your Digital
Lifestyle

PowerBook on
the Go

The last stop on our keyboard tour are the Ctrl, Option, and Apple keys, located to the left of the spacebar. Holding down the Ctrl (pronounced: "control") key while clicking with the trackpad is just like right-clicking in Windows—it reveals a contextual menu.

The Option key is used like the Alt key in Windows to provide added functionality to a keystroke. For example, hold down the Option key and type the number 8. You'll get a bullet symbol instead of the number.

And the Apple key—also called the Command (⌘) key—is used for many keyboard shortcuts. So, as an alternative to using the menu control *File → Print* to print a document, you could use the keyboard shortcut, ⌘-P—hold down the Apple key and type "P". In fact, you'll see the shortcut combination in the drop-down menu if you view *File → Print*. So you always have a handy reference if you forget what the shortcut is.

PowerBook
Fan Book

Rest stop

The PowerBook's beauty is not just skin deep. There are lots of handy shortcuts and sophisticated technology built in to this attractive package. As you work your way through this guide, you'll discover that the PowerBook is as smart as it is attractive.

And speaking of good looking, I show you how to maintain that beautiful body of a computer in the next chapter.

First take a short break to rest your eyes and hands, and then we'll explore cases, screen protectors, and cleaners.

Connecting with
Your PowerBook

**Care and
Feeding**

Getting
Started

Organize
Your Life

Your Digital
Lifestyle

PowerBook on
the Go

The PowerBook enclosure is designed to provide the utmost durability while maintaining its sleek beauty. Apple selected aluminum alloy, then hardened and anodized it to protect the surface from stains, scratches, and discoloration. The aluminum is wrapped around an internal frame for added stability, and the hard drive is rubber mounted to the structure providing a degree of shock resistance for this important component's moving parts.

Even with all of this protection, you shouldn't be too cavalier about how you treat your investment. It's still a computer. There are vulnerable parts such as the LCD viewing screen. And in order to preserve its beauty, you want to protect your PowerBook from the bumps and bruises that often come with everyday life.

In this chapter, I'll show you many accessories that will help you combat the elements of a hostile environment. This array of cases, keyboard protectors, and screen cleaners doesn't cost very much, but they all go a long way toward extending the beauty and functionality of your stylish computer.

Cases

Thanks to its rounded corners, the PowerBook slips easily into a backpack. And that's how many users like to tote 'em around. You have a couple options here. You can buy a backpack especially designed for your computer, or you can use a *sleeve* that protects your PowerBook when you carry it around in a pack you already have now.

One of the advantages of backpacks over standard laptop cases is that they don't necessarily shout, "I have a computer in here!" This is a plus when hanging out in public places.

This rugged STM backpack designed for 15" PowerBooks is made out of water-resistant 600D polyester, features a suspended laptop pouch to protect the PowerBook from impact, plus plenty of room for the rest of your gear. It even has a waterproof zipper for the laptop pouch. The handles and straps are excellent (about $75 www.stmbags.com).

Aside from durable construction and pockets that are easily accessible, one thing I look for in a backpack is a sturdy carrying handle on the top. There are many times when you need to just grab it and go. So a good handle that's comfortable to grip is a necessary feature.

Of the different types of backpacks I've recently reviewed, I like the STM line because their bags function like they were designed by people who actually carry computers around with them. The handle and straps are rugged, there's lots of accessible storage space, and your PowerBook is stashed safely in the middle of lots of padding.

Connecting with
Your PowerBook

**Care and
Feeding**

Getting
Started

Organize
Your Life

Your Digital
Lifestyle

PowerBook on
the Go

If you want to use your existing backpack, I recommend picking up Marware's SportFolio Sleeve. It's very well designed, feels good to the touch, and will protect your PowerBook in the most hostile of luggage environments. You can check out the sleeves at *www.marware.com*. They sell for about $30.

For an innovative twist on the backpack design, take a look at the Back Office by SJ Designs. It opens up to a portable office that literally sits on your lap. When you're finished working, you fold everything up, including your PowerBook, and tote it by the handle or on your back with the optional Mesh Backpack Harness. The Back Office is sturdy and features a good carrying handle.

The Back Office is the ultimate portable workspace
(about $150 *www.laptopoffice.com*).

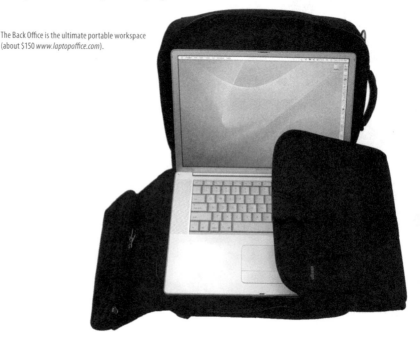

Sometimes backpacks aren't appropriate for the office or your typical business meeting. Those situations require more traditional luggage, such as a briefcase or stylish messenger bag.

Even though briefcases look great in the office, they often don't have as much room for accessories as backpacks. Fortunately, PowerBooks have such good battery life (you don't need to carry extras) and most everything else you need is built right in. You often don't have to lug too many additional components to the office.

One of my favorite briefcases is the Marware Milano executive case. It's designed to protect every corner of your PowerBook, and it looks very classy while doing so. Marware combines high-quality cowhide leather and stainless steel hardware to create a rugged, timeless design. The included strap reduces fatigue while dashing through the airport or across town.

The Marware Milano is luxurious laptop luggage for the executive on the go (about $150 *www.marware.com*).

Connecting with
Your PowerBook

Care and
Feeding

Getting
Started

Organize
Your Life

Your Digital
Lifestyle

PowerBook on
the Go

Messenger bags have become popular in recent years because they include many of the desirable storage features found in backpacks, but have styling that's appropriate in the office as well as the classroom.

Spire makes a great-looking messenger bag, the Endo, with lots of great features for bikers, commuters, and anyone who is looking for a great bag that also happens to accommodate your computer. In addition to its generous array of pockets and pouches, the Endo includes a padded sleeve for your PowerBook that can be carried separately as well as in the larger bag.

Spire's Endo messenger bag is perfect for PowerBook owners who sometimes travel off the beaten path (about $80 *www.spireusa.com*).

Keyboard and screen protectors

One of the most common and heartbreaking hazards to befall a PowerBook is spilling something liquid on its keyboard, usually in the form of coffee or cola.

If this happens to you, shut down the computer, unplug it from the power source, and remove the battery. Then take the PowerBook to your nearest Authorized Apple Dealer or an Apple Store. Often the computer can be saved.

But your heart will beat much easier if you prevent these disasters from happening in the first place. I recommend that you don't keep liquids and food on the same surface as your PowerBook. If you are drinking coffee while working—as I often do—keep your coffee cup as far away as is feasible from the computer.

You might want to investigate a keyboard protector too. My favorite is the Protouch iSkin. When I first read about the iSkin, I was skeptical. Yes, it's an attractive blue translucent skin that goes over your keyboard while you work. But how does it feel while typing? Amazingly good, actually. In fact, if you don't like the normal click-click of keystrokes, the iSkin dampens the chatter of typing too.

The Protouch iSkin helps protect your keyboard from crumbs, dust, dust-bunnies—even liquids. It looks very cool, and feels amazingly good to the touch (about $20 www.iskin.com).

Another problem with keyboards is that they transfer accumulated grime from the keys to the laptop screen when you

Connecting with
Your PowerBook

**Care and
Feeding**

Getting
Started

Organize
Your Life

Your Digital
Lifestyle

PowerBook on
the Go

close the computer. I use a couple of items that help prevent the mucking up of my screen.

One of my absolute favorites is the Radtech ScreensavRz protection cloth. Not only does it provide a protective surface between the keyboard and screen, it's made out of a super-soft Optex fabric that you can also use for polishing. You can even dampen a corner of the cloth to remove pesky oils and fingerprints from the screen's surface. If the ScreensavRz gets soiled over time, just toss it in the washing machine to bring it back to life.

Another approach to screen protection is the Marware Keyboard Cover; made from neoprene, it covers only the keys themselves. This rectangular pad only costs about $7 from *www.marware.com*.

Radtech's ScreensavRz protects your screen from keyboard abrasions, and, thanks to its soft Optex fabric, it's also the perfect polishing cloth for delicate surfaces (about $15 *www.radtech.us*).

Cleaning inside and out

Even with the best care, your PowerBook will need occasional cleaning. I've been using iKlear for years, and their latest kit for the PowerBook includes a 5 oz. spray bottle of cleaner, a micro-chamois polishing cloth, and six Wet/Dry Travel Singles that are perfect for stashing in your PowerBook travel case.

The iKlear spray is amazing stuff. It doesn't contain any alcohol or ammonia to harm your PowerBook, but it cleans wonderfully. After buffing with the micro fiber cloth, the spray leaves a shiny layer of anti-static protection on your LCD screen. You can use it to clean the case too.

The iKlear Cleaning kit is perfect for polishing both the screen and case of your PowerBook (about $20 www.iklear.com).

Connecting with
Your PowerBook

Care and
Feeding

Getting
Started

Organize
Your Life

Your Digital
Lifestyle

PowerBook on
the Go

Rest stop

The accessories in this chapter provide you with everything you need to protect and maintain the outer surfaces of your PowerBook. Now that beauty is assured, it's time to lift the hood and learn a little about the personality inside.

After you finish your online ordering of PowerBook goodies, take a quick rest break because the next three chapters are going to keep you pretty busy. I'm going to take you on a tour of some of the excellent software that Apple has installed on the hard drive, including Mac OS X itself. You'll learn how to quickly configure your PowerBook and start using some of its applications.

The Start of a Beautiful Friendship

2

Connecting with
Your PowerBook

Care and
Feeding

Getting
Started

Organize
Your Life

Your Digital
Lifestyle

PowerBook on
the Go

The first time you press the power button on your PowerBook, Apple greets you with the rather generic Setup Assistant and walks you through the very first steps of making the machine your own. So now what? The computer that sits before you is functional—in fact, it's very functional. But it isn't really *yours* yet. You haven't bonded. Even though it's stunningly beautiful, it's still just like every other PowerBook proudly escorted out of the Apple Store.

When I sit down with new Mac owners, the first thing I do is introduce them to its System Preferences. This is the home for a collection of tools that allow you to personalize your computer.

Imagine for a moment if you could do this with other major purchases in life. What if you could press a button and change the color of your car? Or pull a lever and move the front door of your house from the east side of the building to the west? Not very likely, is it?

But that's why you bought a PowerBook instead of some other less personable computer. After you become familiar with how to adjust key System Preferences, you have the power to adapt your computer to meet not only your functional needs, but your aesthetic ones as well. So we're going to begin the bonding process right here—in the System Preferences. And in less than an hour, you'll make what was once Apple's Power-Book, *your PowerBook*.

System Preferences that matter

The easiest way to access the collection of System Preferences is to locate its icon—the light switch with the Apple logo—on the Dock at the bottom of your screen. If you're in doubt that you've found the correct icon, simply wave your trackpad pointer over it, and the name System Preferences should appear above the icon. Now click it. The light switch will bounce a few times while the application loads, then a window of goodies will appear on your screen.

If for some reason the icon isn't on your Dock, you can always access System Preferences under the Apple icon (🍎) in the top-left corner of the Menu Bar.

Your PowerBook helps you keep track of its various System Preferences by dividing them up into five categories. You're going to learn a little about every preference shown here.

Connecting with
Your PowerBook

Care and
Feeding

**Getting
Started**

Organize
Your Life

Your Digital
Lifestyle

PowerBook on
the Go

Apple has organized the preferences into five categories: Personal, Hardware, Internet & Network, System, and Other. I touch on each preference within those categories. Some of them you'll adjust right away—I label those as *Starter*. Others I'll briefly describe, but you won't be tinkering with them until later because they're not really necessary at this stage; I label those preferences as *Optional*.

I'll make my recommendations for each Starter preference pane, however, feel free to customize on your own. I'll start in the top-left corner and work across and down from there. After you establish settings in a particular pane, click on the Show All icon in the upper-left corner to return to the top-level view of System Preferences. From there, you'll move to the next one in line until you reach the end.

Appearance (Starter)

Here's where you establish the basic look and feel of your PowerBook. I recommend the Blue setting for the overall look, and Gold as the highlight color. Most people prefer keeping the scroll arrows together, and the scroll bar set to Scroll to here. Now jump down to the bottom of the panel and select Medium—best for Flat Panel for font smoothing style, with smoothing turned off for font sizes 8 and smaller. These appearance settings should look good on your PowerBook. Season for taste as needed. To return to the overview of System Preferences, click on the Show All icon in the upper-left corner of the pane.

Desktop & Screensaver (Starter)

One of the easiest ways to distinguish your PowerBook from those of others is via the desktop background screen. In the Windows world they call this the *wallpaper*. When you click on the Desktop button, you're greeted with a variety of patterns to select from. Some are more rectangular in shape—those are designed for your PowerBook. Later, after you've put some of your own digital images in the Pictures folder, you can choose one of those for your desktop background. But for now select one of the many options that Apple has provided for you. Now click on the Screen Saver button and survey the handful of visual gems preloaded into your PowerBook. You can peek at the options in the preview window, but if you want the full experience, hit the Test button. Click your screen again to exit out of the test and return to the preference pane.

I recommend using 30 minutes as the period of inactive time before your screensaver activates. Go to Hot Corners and choose "Start Screen Saver" from the upper-right drop down menu (leave the other three selections blank for now. You'll configure them in future preference panes.) Click OK. Now when you use your trackpad pointer (or mouse) to move to the upper-right corner of the PowerBook screen, the screensaver will begin. Move the pointer again, and the PowerBook will exit the screensaver and you'll return to your normal desktop screen.

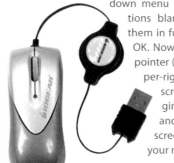

The IoGear USB Memory Mini Mouse 800 is a pocketable high-resolution (800dpi) optical mouse with 32 or 64 MBs of Flash memory. Works great with PowerBooks; just don't forget to eject the Flash drive (by dragging its icon to the trash) before unplugging the mouse (about $50 www.iogear.com).

Dock (Starter)

Control the appearance and functionality of the icons located at the bottom of your screen. Apple calls this the Dock—think of your program icons as little ships, some docked permanently, others just windows stopping by for a while. The settings for Size and Position are self-evident—you can control how big your Dock appears on the screen with Size, and relocate it to the left or right edge of your screen with Position.

If you click the *magnification* box to turn it on, the Dock icons will enlarge when you wave the pointer over them. I also recommend using the the *Minimize function to Scale Effect*. This uses less processor power as files and windows zoom up from the Dock and open on the screen. Just as a note, when you have one of these application windows open, you can *minimize* it (essentially sending it back to the Dock) by clicking the orange button in the upper-left corner of the window. To restore it to full view, click on its Dock image, and it will spring back to life on your screen (though any activity occurring in the window—music playing in an iTunes window for example—will continue while the window is minimized).

Connecting with
Your PowerBook

Care and
Feeding

Getting
Started

Organize
Your Life

Your Digital
Lifestyle

PowerBook on
the Go

Exposé (Starter)

Exposé is one of those delightful joys of Mac computing. With one easy command, it allows you to spread all of your open windows out on your desktop, all the better to easily identify and choose the one you're after. This is particularly handy for people who like to have lots of windows open on smaller laptop screens, such as the 12" PowerBook.

When you open the Exposé preference pane, it will look familiar to you. That's because the top section is the same thing you saw when you clicked on the Hot Corners button in Screen Saver preference. In fact, you'll see that the upper-right drop-down menu is already set!

The upper-right menu is already set for your screensaver, so go ahead and set the lower-right drop-down menu to *All Windows*. This is the Exposé setting that allows you to organize all of the window clutter on your desktop just by dragging the pointer to the lower-right corner. Sometimes you might want to use a keyboard command to do this instead. So go ahead and select F12 from the All Windows drop-down menu in the Keyboard area (as shown in the figure).

To see how it works, run this test. Find the Address Book icon on your Dock and click it; Address Book will launch and open a window. You now have two windows open

on your screen: Address Book and the Exposé preference pane. Drag your pointer to the lower-right corner of the screen and watch what happens. The two open windows shrink in size so you can see both at the same time. Now click on the window you want to bring to the foreground, and Exposé reorganizes your windows! You can do this with as many open windows as you want.

Easily set hot corners and keyboard commands for Exposé.

You can achieve the same effect by pressing the F12 key (you set this to be the case earlier). Either way works; it's just a matter of preference.

Return to the Exposé preference pane and set the lower-left drop-down menu to Desktop and change the Desktop keyboard preference to F11. This clears all of the windows on your screen and allows you to access items on your desktop. Finally, set the upper-left drop-down menu to Application Windows and the corresponding keyboard command to F10. This function is very handy for managing programs that often have many open windows, such as Photoshop. The difference between this setting and All Windows, is that Application Windows only organizes the open windows with that program, such as Photoshop. All Windows organizes every window on your desktop.

After you play with Exposé a bit, you'll discover it's an invaluable tool for managing your limited screen real estate. You can find more information on Apple's web site at *www.apple.com/macosx/features/expose/*.

International (Optional)

If your PowerBook labels are displayed in your native language, you don't need to make any adjustments here now. But you should know that your Macintosh has many languages built in to the operating system, and you can switch among them via this preference pane. For more information, see Apple's web page at *www. apple.com/macosx/features/international/*.

Security (Optional)

Your Mac operating system is a modern relative to robust Unix computers that have been serving universities and enterprise businesses for years. One of the benefits of this heritage is the ability to secure your PowerBook from the prying eyes of others. At the moment, I'm not going to have you change any of the settings in the Security preference pane. But we will return here later after a few other settings have been established. If you want a sneak peek at some more of Security's features, go to *www.apple.com/macosx/features/filevault/*.

Connecting with
Your PowerBook

Care and
Feeding

**Getting
Started**

Organize
Your Life

Your Digital
Lifestyle

PowerBook on
the Go

CDs & DVDs (Optional)

Now we're into the Hardware section of System Preferences. The defaults for CDs & DVDs are good, so you don't have to think about them now. But up the road, if you want a specific action to occur when you insert optical media into your PowerBook, this is the place to make that adjustment.

Displays (Starter)

By the time you get to this preference pane, Mac OS X has identified the hardware in your PowerBook and has configured the Displays preferences properly. However, I think it is very handy to have the shortcut for adjusting Displays appear in the Menu Bar (the very top row of icons on your PowerBook where the Apple logo appears in the upper-left corner). To enable this, check the box labeled *Show displays in the menu bar*. This is particularly useful if you ever connect your PowerBook to an LCD projector or external monitor, and you want to enable *mirroring*. This is a handy control that enables you to see the same image on your PowerBook screen that's being projected or displayed on the external monitor. You can turn mirroring off and on quickly by using the Menu Bar Displays icon instead of having to open System Preferences.

Energy Saver (Starter)

Here's where you get to control when your computer automatically goes to sleep (after a period of inactivity) and when it wakes. These controls are particularly important for laptops that rely on precious battery power.

To reveal the options you have, click on the Show Details button in the lower-right corner. The first important thing to note about this preference pane is that you have separate controls for when the PowerBook is running off the power adapter or the battery (configurable via the Settings for drop-down menu).

Let's start with configuring the power adapter. I recommend that you set the PowerBook to sleep after one hour (both for the computer itself and the display, as shown in the illustration.) Because power isn't really an issue when you're plugged into the wall, there's no need to have your PowerBook go to sleep every time you turn away for a minute to answer the phone. Also, check the box labeled *Put the hard disk(s) to sleep when possible.*

Now configure the settings for battery power. Generally speaking you want to be more conservative here, so start with putting the display to sleep after 15 minutes and see how that works for you. Check the box labeled Show battery status in the menu bar so you can easily monitor your battery while you work.

Here's a cool feature of Mac OS X. The operating system knows when you're using the power adapter or running off battery power, and it automatically chooses the right settings in the Energy Saver preference pane.

Custom energy settings for when the power adapter is plugged in.

You have additional settings in the Schedule and Options panes, but you can leave them alone for the time being. If you ever want to have your PowerBook automatically wake and sleep at a specific time each day, return here to set those parameters.

Keyboard & Mouse (Starter)

Even though it isn't included in the title, this is also the preference pane where you configure your trackpad. The title should really be "Keyboard, Mouse & Trackpad." There are two important areas here that I want you to look at right now. The others you can play with at your convenience.

Click on the Trackpad button to reveal its settings. First, experiment with the tracking and double-clicking speeds until you find settings that are comfortable. Now I'm going to show you something really cool. Check the box labeled Clicking. I think the Clicking box should really be labeled "Tapping" because when it's activated, you can

Connecting with
Your PowerBook

Care and
Feeding

Getting
Started

Organize
Your Life

Your Digital
Lifestyle

PowerBook on
the Go

simply tap the trackpad instead of having to use your thumb to press the trackpad bar. Try it. Instead of using the bar to check the box labeled *Ignore accidental trackpad input*, simply put the pointer over it and tap the trackpad. It will check the box. This is particularly handy when you want to use your PowerBook during meetings and not disturb others with the constant clicking of the trackpad bar.

Here's a tip. Tap twice on the top bar of any open window, and you can minimize it. To bring it back to life, find it on the Dock and tap once.

By the way, leave the box labeled *Ignore accidental trackpad input* checked so that you don't send your pointer flying about the screen if you accidentally brush the trackpad while typing.

For mousing on the go without wires, take a look at the Radtech BT-500 mouse. It communicates with your PowerBook via the Bluetooth technology built-in to your laptop (about $55 *www.radtech.us*).

The other area I want you to visit is Keyboard Shortcuts. Here you'll find a cornucopia of custom settings that you can use to more quickly control your PowerBook. If you like the speed of using the keyboard instead of drop-down menus for certain commands, you'll love this preference pane.

Print & Fax (Starter)

 Apple has made it as easy as possible for you to connect to your printer. Plug in your printer cable to the PowerBook, power it up, and then click the Set Up Printers button in the Printing preference pane. Your PowerBook will launch the Printer Setup Utility and open the Printer List window. Click the Add button and the PowerBook will identify your printer and list it in a window. Once your printer has been located and listed, click on its name once to highlight it and click the Add button. It will then be added to the Printer list and available for work.

There is one "gotcha" to keep an eye on when setting up a printer. You'll notice that there's a drop-down menu in the upper part of the Printer List pane. Make sure that you've selected the correct connection type from that menu. If, for example, you're setting up a USB printer, then USB should be selected from the menu (as shown in the illustration). Otherwise you'll find yourself scratching your head wondering why the computer and printer aren't talking to each other.

You can now make sure that your chosen printer appears automatically in all of your print dialog boxes—just return to the Printing preference pane and choose your printer from the drop-down menu labeled *Selected printer in Print Dialog:*.

Make sure you have the correct connection type selected, or your computer and printer won't be able to talk. Here, I've chosen USB for my inkjet printer.

If you add a new printer that you want to use as the default printer, return to the Print & Fax preference pane and choose the new printer from the Selected printer in the Print Dialog drop-down menu.

You have other options here too, such as sharing your printer over a network and sending Fax documents directly from your PowerBook. You can learn more about sending and receiving faxes by visiting Apple's web page: *www.apple.com/macosx/features/faxing/*. You can also learn more about printing by visiting: *www.apple.com/macosx/features/printing/*.

Sound (Starter)

There are lots of goodies in this preference pane that enable you to control audio input and output. But for today, I'm going to have you set two quick preferences. The first, in the Sound Effects preference pane, is the alert sound. You have a list of interesting noises you can use as your system alert. Make sure your output volume is turned up, and then simply click on an alert sound to preview it. Once you find your favorite, just leave it highlighted.

Connecting with
Your PowerBook

Care and
Feeding

Getting
Started

Organize
Your Life

Your Digital
Lifestyle

PowerBook on
the Go

While you're in the neighborhood, check the box labeled *Show volume in menu bar*. This is an extremely handy way to adjust the volume while working, without having to open the Sound preference window.

More advanced options in Sound include selecting the source of audio input, such as using your PowerBook's internal microphone to record your voice. You have output alternatives too if you want to pipe sound out of your PowerBook into a USB speaker system. If you want to learn more about the advanced audio technology built into Mac OS X, visit Apple's web page at *www.apple.com/macosx/features/audio/*.

.Mac (Optional)

This preference pane gives you direct access to Apple's online service called .Mac. If you have an account already, you can enter your name and password here so your PowerBook can connect to .Mac when necessary, such as when publishing a Web page in iPhoto. If you don't have an account and are interested in the service, click the Sign Up button for a 60-day free trial. You can find out lots more about .Mac by visiting *www.mac.com*.

Network (Starter)

This is one of the most important areas in System Preferences. Network is where you establish your connection with the outside world via the Internet. Depending on the accessories you included with your PowerBook, you have the option of establishing a network connection via dial-up modem, Ethernet—DSL or cable modem, or AirPort 802.11 wireless (optional AirPort card required).

At any time you can check your current connection to the Internet and other configured connection options by choosing Automatic from the Location drop-down menu and Network Status from the Show menu. Your PowerBook will display all the connections you've enabled and indicate whether they are live or not.

But what if you haven't established any connections? First decide how you want to connect—modem, Ethernet, or AirPort. If modem or Ethernet is your choice, then plug the appropriate cable into your PowerBook and the other end into your phone jack, broadband router, or Ethernet hub.

The Wacom Graphire3 pen and tablet gives you more control than a standard optical mouse, and is great for editing digital photos and creating artwork. And for times when a mouse is more convenient, it includes one of those too (about $99 *www.wacom.com*).

Now click on the Assist me button at the bottom of the Network preferences pane, and your PowerBook will walk you through the procedure of connecting to the Internet. Be sure to have all of your account information handy, such as username and password. Within minutes, the Network Setup Assistant will have you online able to access web pages and email.

Return to this preference pane in the future when you want to add more network connections, or customize existing ones. It's also a helpful place to see if you are indeed connected, and if so, by which method. You can learn much more about networking on the Apple web site at *www.apple.com/macosx/features/networking/*.

QuickTime (Optional)

QuickTime is the foundation underlying much of Apple's digital media technology. It enables your PowerBook to play movies and listen to audio. Fortunately for you, Apple has configured this functionality for you. Up the road however, you may want to tailor some of the settings, such as whether or not to play downloaded movies automatically. When that time comes, return to this preference pane to customize your QuickTime settings. If you want to learn more about QuickTime's capabilities, visit *www.apple.com/macosx/features/quicktime/*.

Connecting with
Your PowerBook

Care and
Feeding

**Getting
Started**

Organize
Your Life

Your Digital
Lifestyle

PowerBook on
the Go

Sharing (Optional)

Apple has included lots of services within the Sharing preferences pane. One of the most commonly used functions is the ability to share an Internet connection (established via modem or Ethernet) with others using AirPort; this is handy in a café or hotel room where phone lines or broadband Internet are scarce (and costly). You can find these settings under the Internet tab in the Sharing preference pane.

For the most part, however, you won't need to spend much time here in the early stages of your PowerBook experience. Just keep in mind that this is the place to go if you decide you want to share your printer or Internet connection with others nearby. Also here is one of the more intriguing functions built into Mac OS X—Personal Web Sharing. You can literally serve a web site on your local network or the Internet by configuring this preference pane. If you're curious and want to know more, visit *www.apple.com/macosx/features/websharing/*.

Accounts (Starter)

Here's a very important, and often overlooked area, in the process of personalizing your PowerBook. Apple gets you started during the initial setup process by establishing an Admin account for you. But you have many options beyond the basic configuration, and I want to show you a few of them now.

First, this is your PowerBook, so you are considered the administrator. That means that your password is often required to load new software or make changes to the system itself. In the Password preference pane you'll see this basic information you entered during the initial setup of your PowerBook. If you need to change it, here's where that happens. You can also access your Address Book card here by clicking the Edit button.

While you're here though, click on Login Options in the lower-left corner of this pane. Make sure the button labeled *List of users* is enabled, and leave the other check boxes blank. Click on your name to exit this area.

Many people overlook Login Options in the lower-left corner of the Accounts preference pane. But this is where you make sure automatic login is turned off so you can keep your PowerBook secure.

After you have the Accounts preferences set up, jump back to the Security preference pane and enable password protection.

You can change the icon associated with your name in the Picture preference pane. For the moment, don't worry about the Security and Startup Items pane. We are going to add some security to your PowerBook, but I'm going to take you to a different area to do so.

Go back to the Password pane and reenter your secret code in both the Password and Verify panes. Make sure you remember your password! It is vital to the security on your PowerBook.

Now click on the Show All icon in the upper-left corner to return to the main view of System Preferences. With your password fresh in your mind, we're going to return to the Security preference pane and change one setting. Check the box labeled *Require password to wake this computer from sleep or screen saver.*

Doing this allows you to secure your PowerBook from prying eyes by simply activating the screensaver or putting it to sleep. When you activate it again, your PowerBook will ask you for your password before proceeding. This is a much faster way to secure your computer when you step away for a few minutes than having to shut down or

Connecting with
Your PowerBook

Care and
Feeding

**Getting
Started**

Organize
Your Life

Your Digital
Lifestyle

PowerBook on
the Go

PowerBook
Fan Book

log out completely. If you decide you don't like this level of security, then simply return to the Security preference pane and uncheck this box.

One last note about the Accounts preference pane—if you decide you want to allow another user to have his own environment on your PowerBook, you can do so by clicking the "+" box in the lower-left corner. This allows you to establish a new account. You have the option of allowing the other user administrator rights. Think this through carefully before making your decision. Other users with administrator rights can change any overall aspect of your PowerBook.

Date and Time (Starter)

 There's nothing terribly fancy here, but there are a few things I want to point out. First, if you have an Internet connection established, you can synchronize your PowerBook with the government's super accurate atomic clock. Just check the box labeled *Set Date & Time automatically* in the Date & Time preference pane. Your PowerBook will connect with the timekeeping web site and set its time precisely.

Now jump over to the Clock preference pane. Check the box labeled *Show the date and time*, and then play with the various options available. Most people display the clock digitally in the Menu Bar. But, this is *your PowerBook*, and you can customize it to suit your tastes.

Software Update (Starter)

In my opinion, Software Update is another terrific perk of owning a Mac, especially if you have a fast Internet connection such as DSL or cable. In the first pane labeled Update Software, you can set the frequency at which your PowerBook connects with Apple's servers to compare its software with current versions Apple has made available. If something newer is ready, your PowerBook will then list all of the updates that are relevant to your configuration, and give you the option of selecting which ones you want to download. Software Update even installs the updates for you after they've been loaded on to your computer!

If you're connected to the Internet right now, click on the Check Now button to manually initiate the process. Keep in mind however, that you need to have your administrator's password handy, and that you often have to restart your PowerBook after installing certain types of software. Generally speaking, I prefer not to have my Mac automatically check for updates, so I leave the box labeled *Check for updates* unchecked, and then I manually log on using the Check Now button.

If you want to review recent software downloads, click on the Installed Updates label to see a list of installed updates. You can learn more about this great feature by visiting: *www.apple.com/macosx/upgrade/softwareupdates.html*.

Speech (Optional)

Your PowerBook ships with sophisticated speech recognition and spoken word technology built right in. This software is particularly handy if you find it necessary to speak basic commands instead of typing them on the keyboard. You can also have your PowerBook speak alerts to you by configuring this capability in the Spoken User Interface preference pane. Apple has published an informative web page about this technology: *www.apple.com/macosx/features/speech/*.

Startup Disk (Optional)

Sometimes power users like to partition their hard drives and install a different version of system software on the other partition. The Startup Disk preference pane is a handy way to tell the computer which system software to use when the power button is turned on. If you're content with just using one version of Mac OS X, you can probably skip this area for now.

Universal Access (Optional)

If you have difficulties reading normal size computer type, hearing system alerts, or using the keyboard or trackpad, there are some useful enhancements in the Universal Access preference pane. You can refer to Apple's web page on Universal Access for more information: *www.apple.com/macosx/features/universalaccess/*.

You've now completed your first tour of the PowerBook's System Preferences. What was once a stock laptop, configured in an Apple factory, is now one step closer to becoming your personal computing partner. Before we move on however, I still have a few more tips for you.

Connecting with
Your PowerBook

Care and
Feeding

**Getting
Started**

Organize
Your Life

Your Digital
Lifestyle

PowerBook on
the Go

First, notice that Apple has put what it believes to be the most commonly used preferences at the top of the System Preferences window. But you might have others that you prefer reside there instead. To customize this top menu area, just drag and drop preference icons in and out of this area. To remove an icon, for example, simply grab it and drag it out of the area. It will vaporize in a cloud of smoke. (Don't worry, it's still below in its normal place with the others; you haven't deleted it all together—you've simply removed a pointer to the original from the top menu area.)

By the same token, to add a favorite preference to the top area, drag it up there and position it where you want. You can also move existing icons around, ordering them in any way that pleases you.

Now, remember when we first launched System Preferences? We did that from the Dock at the bottom of your PowerBook's viewing screen. But if you'd rather free up the Dock space for other icons, you can drag the System Preferences icon off the Dock, and it too will vaporize in a cloud of smoke.

I mentioned this earlier, but I'll touch on it again—you can always launch Preferences by clicking on the Apple icon in the upper-left corner of your screen and choosing System Preferences from the drop-down menu.

It's time to take a deep breath and admire your handiwork. In less than an hour you've seized control of the situation. It feels great, doesn't it? But we're just getting warmed up. Now it's time to explore the vast universe we call the Internet.

PowerBook
Fan Book

Cruising the Internet superhighway

If you already established an Internet connection by configuring the Network preference pane (on page 22), then you're ready to explore the Web, exchange email, and send instant messages via iChat. Apple has preloaded these programs on your PowerBook. You can find them, along with other preloaded software, in the Applications folder. (If you haven't been there yet, double-click the hard drive icon in the upper-right corner of your PowerBook's screen. You'll see the Applications folder inside.)

Internet Connect

Internet Connect is a hidden gem in the Applications folder that makes getting online as simple as clicking a button. Double-click on its icon to launch the program.

Internet Connect uses the information you entered previously in the Network preferences pane to get you online quickly.

Connecting with
Your PowerBook

Care and
Feeding

Getting
Started

Organize
Your Life

Your Digital
Lifestyle

PowerBook on
the Go

PowerBook
Fan Book

Internet Connect works hand in hand with the network configuration you did earlier in the Network preference pane. Choose your method for getting online, such as internal modem, as shown in the illustration. Select your configuration from the drop-down menu that you set up earlier in the Network preference pane. Most likely, Mac OS X has already figured out that you want to use it and has selected it for you.

Make sure you've connected the cable from your PowerBook to the phone jack, and then press the blue Connect button. If all of your information was entered correctly, you'll be online in a matter of minutes.

Remember, though, Internet Connect won't be of much value until you enter the details of your configuration—whether it be dial-up modem, DSL, cable modem, or AirPort wireless—in the Network System Preference pane.

America Online subscribers don't have to configure Network or Internet Connect to start using the service. The AOL software will walk you through the process in just a few minutes.

The Safari browser

Once you're online, it's time to launch a web browser and check your favorite site. Go back to the Applications folder and double-click on Safari (or click the the Safari compass icon in your Dock). This is Apple's web browser, and it's fantastic.

Safari looks similar to many other browsers you may have used, only it's prettier! You can search Google directly by entering your search words in the Google field in the upper-right corner of Safari. Also note that Safari supports tabbed browsing, so you don't have to open a new window for every new web site you want to browse.

Connecting with
Your PowerBook

Care and
Feeding

Getting
Started

Organize
Your Life

Your Digital
Lifestyle

PowerBook on
the Go

The first thing to do is go to Safari's preferences (*Safari → Preferences*) and click on the Bookmarks icon. Check the box labeled *Include Bookmarks Bar*. This adds a menu bar in the top part of Safari's window that allows you to store your favorite Web address for easy access. To add a Web address to the Bookmarks Bar, grab the icon next to the web address and drag it to the Bookmarks Bar.

After a while, you may want to do a little housekeeping with your bookmarks. Click on the open book icon at the left end of the Bookmarks Bar, and you're presented with a window that allows you to reorganize your entire collection. When you're finished, click on the open book again to return to normal browsing.

Now back to Safari's Preferences. Click on the Tabs icon, and check the boxes labeled *Enable Tabbed Browsing* and *Always show tab bar*. This creates another row beneath your Bookmarks Bar. Now, instead of managing multiple browser windows (which isn't much fun on a small PowerBook screen), you can instead create a new tab within your existing browser window to load a new Web page. More tabs are created by going to *File → New Tab* or by using the keystroke ⌘-T. I often have five or six web pages open at once within a single browser window using Tabs. To jump from one page to the next, I click on the appropriate tab.

You can also use shortcuts for these types of maneuvers. The keystroke combination ⌘-shift-left arrow will jump you to the next tab to the left, and ⌘-shift-right arrow jumps you to the next tab to the right.

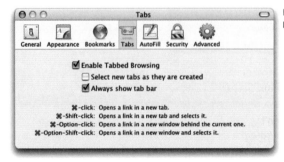

Enable tabbed browsing in Safari's
preferences window (*Safari → Preferences*).

Online shoppers will also be interested in the AutoFill icon in Safari's preferences. Check the box labeled *Using info from my Address Book card*. If you don't already have a card filled out with your personal information, then click on the Edit button and Safari will take you there so you can do so.

I also suggest that you add the AutoFill icon to Safari's top menu bar. That way, when you encounter a Web form online asking for your personal information, all you have to do is click the AutoFill icon and Safari will complete the form for you. You can add the AutoFill icon to Safari's menu bar by clicking on View, (at the top of the screen) then checking AutoFill from the drop-down menu.

One other Safari tip: you can block those annoying pop-up windows that some sites torture you with by going to the Safari menu and selecting *Block Pop-Up Windows*.

The Default Web Browser Trick

Mac OS X supports many excellent web browsers in addition to Safari, such as Firefox (*www.mozilla.org/products/firefox/*). So what do you do if you want to change your default browser from Safari to Firefox? Believe it or not, you make that setting in Safari's preferences, under the General tab. At the top of the General preference pane is a drop-down menu labeled *Default Web Browser*. Make your selection there and you're set.

You're now ready to enjoy exploring the Web with your PowerBook. As you become more comfortable, experiment with other settings in this browser. For example, if you go to the View drop-down menu, you'll see two controls labeled *Make Text Bigger* and *Make Text Smaller*. These two commands let you adjust the way text is rendered on a particular web page. Safari is full of goodies like these. You just have to play a little to discover them.

And while you're browsing, don't forget to check out Apple's web page dedicated to this application at *www.apple.com/safari/*.

Connecting with
Your PowerBook

Care and
Feeding

**Getting
Started**

Organize
Your Life

Your Digital
Lifestyle

PowerBook on
the Go

Mail call!

For the online community, email is both a curse and blessing. The curse is, or course, spam—that mountain of unwanted mail that piles up in your inbox each week. The blessing is that email is still an efficient vehicle for legitimate written communication.

Apple's Mail application identifies potential spam for you by highlighting it in brown. You can also look for older mail by entering the subject or the person in the search field in the upper-right corner.

PowerBook
Fan Book

You most likely have an email account already. Regardless of whether you're using America Online (AOL), Earthlink, or the services of a local Internet Service Provider (ISP), your new PowerBook can handle them all. For commercial services such as AOL, simply download the latest version of the email *client*, that is the program that allows you to connect to the service, enter your username and password, and you're up and running.

If you have a local ISP and have been using a standalone email client such as Microsoft's Entourage or Outlook, or Eudora, this might be a good time to give Apple's email program a look. It's simply referred to as *Mail*, and you can find it in your Applications folder or residing on your Dock.

Mail is a robust email client with an intelligent junk mail filter. I'm going to take you on a quick test drive and let you decide if it's a good tool for you.

First open Mail's preferences (*Mail → Preferences*). Click on the Accounts icon so you can enter your account information. Choose Account Type from its drop-down window. Your options are .Mac, POP, IMAP, and Exchange. If you don't know which of these applies to your account, it's most likely POP. The exception might be if you have a .Mac account. Those are usually IMAP.

And that brings up a good point. People who have .Mac accounts and enter their information in the .Mac System Preference pane, will discover that their email account is automatically configured for them in Mail. This is one of the areas where Mac OS X saves you having to enter the same information twice.

The Mail preference window with a .Mac account entered. You can add additional email accounts by clicking on the "+" button in the lower-left corner.

Connecting with
Your PowerBook

Care and
Feeding

**Getting
Started**

Organize
Your Life

Your Digital
Lifestyle

PowerBook on
the Go

Add additional accounts by clicking on the "+" button in the lower-left corner of Mail preferences. Enter the label you want for this account in the Description field, plus your email address and your name. Then add incoming and outgoing server addresses, your username, and your password. If you don't remember this information, you can get it from your ISP.

Now click on the Advanced tab. Remember, you're just taking this application for a test drive, so make sure the box labeled *Remove copy from server after retrieving a message* is not checked. That way your mail still resides on its server, even after you download it here. If you decide you don't like Apple's Mail program, you can go back to your previous email client and retrieve all your messages.

Before you download mail, I want you to go to one other area in preferences. Click on the Junk Mail icon and check the box labeled *Enable Junk Mail filtering*. Also click the button next to leave in my Inbox, but indicate it is Junk Mail (Training). This will give you a look at how this application deals with spam. You can leave all of the other boxes in this preference pane checked.

Click on the red Close button in the upper-left corner of preferences, and Mail will ask you to save this information. Do so.

Make sure you're connected to the Internet, and click on the Get Mail icon in the main view of the Mail window. Your PowerBook will go to work and grab all the messages that are available on the server. Some of the messages will be colored light brown. Those were determined to be spam. Others will be in black text. Mail considers those legitimate messages. You can double-click on any message to read it.

What if a piece of spam was incorrectly labeled as a legitimate message (black text)? Simply click on it once to highlight it, then click on the Junk Mail icon next to Get Mail. The color of the message text label will change from black to light brown. That email is now considered spam. What's interesting about Apple's mail program is that it pays attention to what you consider legitimate mail and what you denote as spam. It actually learns your preferences and gets better at sorting the junk from the good stuff.

Once you feel that Mail understands your spam preferences, you can take it out of Junk Mail Training mode by returning to preferences, clicking on the Junk Mail icon, and clicking the button next to the label *Move it to the Junk mailbox (Automatic)*. Mail will create a Junk mail box for you and put the spam in there. You can decide to review it or delete as necessary. But you won't have the spam mixed in with the legitimate messages.

.Mac Email from Anywhere

Did you know that you can check your .Mac mail account without ever opening your Mail application? It's simple. In Safari type the web address: *www.apple.com/email*. If you're not already logged into your .Mac account, you'll be asked to do so. Once logged in, you'll be able to sort, read, and reply to all your correspondence right there in your Web browser, even if you're on someone else's computer!

This is just a taste of Apple's Mail program. You have lots of other viewing and composing options. But because dealing with spam is such a big issue these days, I thought this little test drive using the Junk Mail function would enable you to best judge this email client. All of your mail is still on the server. So if you don't like Apple's Mail program, you can always go back to your previous email client and download the messages as you did before.

You can learn more about Apple's Mail application by visiting their web page dedicated to this program at *www.apple.com/macosx/features/mail/*.

Connecting with
Your PowerBook

Care and
Feeding

**Getting
Started**

Organize
Your Life

Your Digital
Lifestyle

PowerBook on
the Go

PowerBook
Fan Book

38

Conversing with others using iChat

Instant messaging (IM) is truly one of the joys of Internet connectivity. You can chat via text in real time with the person in a cubicle down the hall, or with a friend on the other side of the continent. Apple's iChat application is an excellent instant messaging client. And I'm going to provide you with a brief introduction.

You can find iChat in your Applications folder. After you've launched it, open its preferences (*iChat → Preferences*) and click on the Accounts icon. All you have to do is enter your existing AIM screen name and password. If you have a .Mac account, you can use that username instead.

iChat shows you all of your buddies who are currently online. And it even lets you know if they're available for voice conversation by showing a telephone icon next to their name.

Now click on the Messages icon and select your balloon and font colors. You have some other options in this window, but you can come back to those later. Close preferences by clicking on the red button in the upper-left corner.

Make sure you're connected to the Internet, and then select *Log in to AIM* from the iChat drop-down menu at the top of your screen. Within seconds all of your buddies will appear in a window ready to converse. Simply double-click on a name to open an IM window and start typing your message.

So let's have some fun. Go to the upper-right corner of your Buddy List window and click on the picture icon. Another window will open that's labeled *Recent Pictures*. Click on Edit Picture to reveal the Buddy Picture window. You can drag a favorite image of yourself here, and that picture will be displayed to others conversing with you via iChat. After you add a shot you like, click on the Set button. Look! Your picture is now in the Buddy List window.

Click on the Available label that's beneath your screen name. This sets your online status so others know if it's a good time or not to "ping" you. If you don't like the standard choices there, you can create your own, such as "Cooking dinner" by selecting the Custom label. Enter in your new status, and it will replace the existing one. Plus iChat adds it to your existing list so you can easily use it again.

iChat is just full of goodies like this. I want to show you just one more now (before we move on to other things) that's perfect for PowerBook users. Not only can you type instant messages, you can speak them too! Yes, iChat enables regular audio conversations just like the phone. Your PowerBook has a built-in microphone and speakers, so all you have to do is find a buddy who also has iChat with audio enabled, and you can invite them to a conversation. How can you tell if they're able to "talk"? If the person has a telephone icon next to their name, they're capable.

Just click once on their name to highlight it, and then click on the phone icon at the bottom of your buddy list window. (Make sure your sound is turned up so you can hear the person when he or she responds.) iChat will invite the person to an audio conversation. If he or she accepts, you simply start talking. The PowerBook microphone will pick up your voice and transmit it over the Internet to the other person.

This function works best if you have a solid broadband Internet connection, such as DSL or cable. But if your modem dial-up connection is reliable, it can work too for audio. Also, most people consider it polite to send the recipient a text message first inquiring about conversing by voice. That way your buddy has the opportunity to state if he or she would like to talk.

iChat has lots of other great features too, such as direct messaging with buddies over a local area network, and using the iSight web cam (pictured on the following page) for video chat. You can explore these and much more by visiting Apple's iChat AV web page at *www.apple.com/ichat/*.

Connecting with
Your PowerBook

Care and
Feeding

Getting
Started

Organize
Your Life

Your Digital
Lifestyle

PowerBook on
the Go

Ah, that wonderful feeling of control

You've certainly covered a lot of ground in just one chapter. Already you should be feeling much more in tune with your PowerBook, even in control to some degree. If you never went beyond using this machine to connect with others via the Internet, it would be a valuable partner in your day-to-day endeavors.

But there's more to discover. So much more. In the next chapter, we'll get organized using Apple's Address Book, iCal, and Stickies.

Apple's iSight is a high quality webcam that enables you to broadcast video as well as audio when using iChat. You need a broadband connection though (about $149 www.apple.com).

Organize Your Life

3

Connecting with
Your PowerBook

Care and
Feeding

Getting
Started

Organize
Your Life

Your Digital
Lifestyle

PowerBook on
the Go

We all have our own techniques for remembering where we have to be, who we have to call, and what we have to do—they just aren't very good. This information is seldom maintained in one central location. Our "system" normally consists of ignored wall calendars, fallen yellow stickies, and unclear phone numbers scribbled on the back of business cards. Yet, somehow we survive. It isn't pretty. And it certainly isn't efficient.

Your PowerBook presents a new opportunity for organization. In this chapter, I'm going to cover three simple applications that reside on your hard drive that can change, or at least organize, your life—Address Book, iCal, and Stickies. They can help you stay on top of the important information that keeps you connected and on time.

Better yet, if you use mobile devices such as a palmOne organizer, smartphone, or even a Windows-based Pocket PC, your PowerBook can "talk" to these devices and keep them updated with the data you've stored on your computer. And if that hasn't caused your eyes to well up with joy, how about the fact that you can back up all of your personal information to protect yourself in case something bad ever happens to your computer, your organizer, or both.

Yes, there is hope for a more organized, efficient life. So, go gather up all those calendars, sticky notes, business cards, and dog-eared little black books, and let's get it together.

Manage contacts with Address Book

Most likely, Address Book is the first item you'll see when you open your Applications folder. It's also sitting on your Dock, just waiting for your names, phone numbers, addresses, email accounts, IM handles, and Web URLs. Beneath its simple exterior lies a powerful database that can store, sort, and transfer every bit of personal information you need to manage.

The Address Book window is divided into three columns. On the left side is Group, which contains the master library of addresses labeled All, and any custom collections you put together. The center column contains the name of each record. When you click on a record name, its contents are displayed in the right window.

Connecting with
Your PowerBook

Care and
Feeding

Getting
Started

Organize
Your Life

Your Digital
Lifestyle

PowerBook on
the Go

You have two options at this point. You can import existing data from another contact manager such as Palm Desktop, or you can start entering information by hand. Neither task is particularly enjoyable, but as you slave away you can comfort yourself by thinking this is the last time you'll ever have to do this.

The Address Book interface has three columns. On the left is Group. In the beginning, it has only three entries there: All, Directories, and Last Import. All displays every entry in your database. We can put Directories and Last Import on the back burner for now.

The next column is labeled Name. Here's where you add and review all of the people and organizations in your collection. Start by adding an entry for you. Why not? It's your address book. Plus, Mac OS X uses your Me card in a variety of helpful ways. For instance, if you want to use the AutoFill function in the Safari Web browser (see Chapter 2 for more on Safari), it uses your Me card to complete those tedious Web forms. This is a good illustration of the Mac's interconnectivity. Filling out an address card now will help you shop faster later.

Click the "+" button at the bottom of the center column, and you're greeted with an information view in the right column containing many blank fields waiting for you to complete. Enter your first name in the First field, and then hit the tab button to move to the next. Each time you hit the tab button, you move one field forward. Hold down the Shift key and hit the tab button, and you move one field backwards.

PowerBook
Fan Book

Deleting Entries

When you import data from other organizers such as the Palm Desktop, this is a good time to "clean house" and delete those entries that are no longer applicable, such as a former girlfriend who has since married, changed her name, and moved from her apartment to a house. To do so, make sure All is selected under the Group column, go to the address card in the center column, highlight it by clicking on it once, and then hit the delete key. Address Book will ask you if you're sure you want to delete the card. Click Yes, and it's gone.

Add all of your personal information. If you need to add more fields—maybe you have lots of phone numbers—click on the green "+" button and Address Book pops out another blank field for you.

After you've entered everything about you (there's more than you thought, isn't there?), click the Edit button again to save the information. Then go to *Card → Make This My Card*. You'll see that the icon changes from a business card to a silhouette of a person. That person is you.

Speaking of pictures, you can add an image to any Address Book entry by dragging it to the image box next to the name. But make sure the picture isn't too big, or you'll only be able to fit an eyeball in there. I've found that pictures about 80 x 80 pixels in size seem to work pretty well.

After you've populated your Address Book database, it's a good idea to back it up so you'll never have to do this tedious work again. You may also want to back up before making extensive changes in the future, just in case you make a mistake and want to go back to the way it was.

All you have to do is choose *File → Back Up Database*, and then select a location for the file. I recommend that you create a new folder (*File → New Folder*) in your Documents folder titled *Address Book Backups*, and save it there. To be extra safe, copy this file to an external hard drive or burn it to CD. That way, if your hard drive crashes, heaven forbid, you won't lose your data.

Address Book can also communicate directly with many Bluetooth-enabled devices. The Nokia 6600 phone can receive entries directly from Address Book. That way you'll never be without a phone number when you need it (about $450 www.nokia.com).

Connecting with
Your PowerBook

Care and
Feeding

Getting
Started

Organize
Your Life

Your Digital
Lifestyle

PowerBook on
the Go

To restore your Address Book from a backup file, go to *File → Revert to Database Backup*, and navigate to the file you saved in your Documents folder. You are now back in business.

There are many, helpful functions in this application. I suggest you explore the Help file (under Help at the top of the menu) to learn more about Address Book. You can add this data to your Palm organizer, many of the latest smartphones, and a host of other applications.

Some of my favorite Address Book functions are printing labels and sending SMS messages. You can learn more about these goodies by visiting Apple's web page: *www.apple.com/macosx/features/addressbook/.*

The right place at the right time with iCal

I keep iCal and Address Book side by side on the Dock. If Address Book is your right hand of organization, keeping you in touch with people, then iCal is the left hand reminding you when and where to meet them. It's your electronic appointment book and planning calendar.

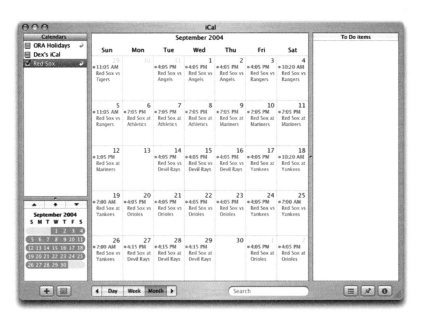

iCal lists your various calendar types (such as work and home) in the far left column. The center window displays the Day, Week, or Month view, as controlled by the tool bar beneath this middle pane. The right column helps you keep track of your To Do list.

Connecting with
Your PowerBook

Care and
Feeding

Getting
Started

**Organize
Your Life**

Your Digital
Lifestyle

PowerBook on
the Go

Like Address book, you have two basic options for adding information to iCal. You can import your appointments from another application, such as Entourage or Palm Desktop, or you can start fresh and type in the things you have scribbled on bits of paper and free calendars from the local bank.

Importing is pretty straightforward. Go to *File → Import*, and you're presented with three options: Import an iCal file, vCal file, or Entourage data. Chances are the first option isn't much use to you unless you have iCal on another Mac. In that case, you could use the Export command to dump the data out of that calendar, and then use Import here to load it.

If anything, odds are higher that you're coming from another calendaring program all together. If it's Microsoft's Entourage, you can export an Entourage archive then import that data into iCal. In your Entourage export options dialog box, check the fields Tasks, Notes, and Calendar events. Entourage will create a tidy archive for you that iCal can understand.

Palm Desktop provides the *vCal* export option, which is a standard format among some calendar programs. When you export your appointments from Palm Desktop to this format, iCal can grab that information and display it just like on your Palm calendar.

The palmOne Treo is a cell phone combined with a Palm organizer. You can synchronize your iCal calendars with the Treo's own calendar program. You can sync with Address Book, too!

With either import method, there's always some clean up. Set aside time to go through your calendar and tidy up a bit. But this is still faster than reentering each appointment by hand.

If you don't have an existing calendar program, you need to start where you are—with this week's appointments. Open iCal, and you'll see that you're once again presented with a three-column window. The left column is where you manage multiple calendars. For now, you're going to start with just one. Give the default calendar name a personal one by double-clicking on it twice to highlight it, and then entering the new name.

You'll notice a mini calendar at the bottom of the third column. This provides you with an overview of the month. You can navigate to any point in time by clicking on individual days or weeks, and iCal will take you there, displaying the larger view in the middle column. You can also use the mini calendar's up and down arrows to go backward and forward in time. The middle diamond always brings you back to today. If you don't like the mini calendar, you can click on the calendar icon beneath it to hide it.

iCal's busy left corner. The mini calendar is actually a navigation tool. Click on the diamond, and it takes you to today. The down arrow moves you forward a month, and the up arrow moves you backward. You can control your views with the Day – Week – Month bar and move backward and forward with those arrows, too.

Connecting with
Your PowerBook

Care and
Feeding

Getting
Started

**Organize
Your Life**

Your Digital
Lifestyle

PowerBook on
the Go

The middle column is your appointment work area. You have three views to choose from: Day, Week, and Month. Select the view you want by using the labeled buttons at the bottom of the column. The arrows on both sides of the buttons move you backward and forward in time.

We'll work in the Month view for now, but the techniques I'll describe work in the other views too. In the Month view, to add a new appointment, simply double-click in the appropriate day. You'll see highlighted text that reads, "New Event." Give it a label by typing in what you want to do on that day.

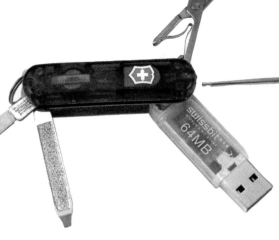

If you want to take your calendars on the road, but leave your PowerBook at home, check out this handy Swiss Memory USB device. Not only does it feature a LED light, pen, scissors, and knife, it contains a 64MB USB drive that works with any modern Mac or PC. Open any monthly calendar in iCal, chose *File → Print* from the menu bar, and then click on the Save as PDF button. iCal will create a PDF file of your calendar (that can be read on any computer). Just copy the file to your Swiss Memory USB, and you can carry it with you whereever you go. There is even a "flight safe" model that doesn't have a knife or scissors (about $65 from ThinkGeek.com).

You'll also notice that you get a pop-up window that allows you to add some specifics about the appointment. This is called the Show Info window. You can change any of the fields, such as when your appointment starts and ends, by clicking on them and entering the information. You'll also see an area to add notes about the appointment. It's a very handy place to jot ideas associated with the appointment itself—such as "Don't order the chicken salad at this place because it almost killed me last time."

If you want to change any specifics of an appointment, you can recall the Show Info display by clicking once on the appointment to highlight it, then click on the *i* icon in the lower-right corner of the iCal interface.

I personally like to see the actual appointment times in the main body of month view, rather than having to display Show Info to see the specifics of the event. To turn this feature on, go to Preferences (*iCal → Preferences*) and check the box labeled, *Show time in month view*.

The right-hand column is your To Do list. You can toggle the visibility of the To Do column by clicking on the thumbtack icon in the lower-right corner of iCal's window. To add a new To Do item, just double-click any blank space in the column (or type ⌘-K) and you'll get a highlighted label titled, *New To Do*. Type your task, and you're set. It's added to the list with a checkbox next to it. You can control the organization of these tasks by going back to Preferences and setting the parameters that best suit your organizational style.

iCal on Your Dock

You can move the iCal icon to any place you want on your Dock by clicking and dragging it to a new location. But have you noticed that its date changes daily when you have the application open? Yes, iCal has a "smart" dock icon. It displays today's date whenever the application is open, even if you have it minimized and out of view. So why does it return to July 17 when you restart your PowerBook? That's its birthday—the day iCal was released.

Connecting with
Your PowerBook

Care and
Feeding

Getting
Started

Organize
Your Life

Your Digital
Lifestyle

PowerBook on
the Go

PowerBook
Fan Book

The last button I want to point out is Search; it's to the left of the thumbtack in the bottom-right corner of iCal. Click it to reveal a pane of recent search results. To look for an appointment that you can't remember when you made it, type in a word that should be in its description in the Search field at the bottom of iCal's interface. All the instances of that word will show up in the Search Result window. Click on the result that you were looking for, and iCal takes you to that appointment. Another disaster averted!

Keep in mind that the Help menu in iCal will introduce you to additional capabilities. I encourage you to take a few moments to look around in there. But for the time being, you've taken the first steps to organizing your daily, weekly, and even monthly schedules. If you use a Palm organizer, you can synchronize this information with your handheld device using iSync (see Apple's web site for more information about iSync: *http:// www.apple.com/isync/*).

One last note about iCal. If you maintain your calendar faithfully, it contains lots of important information that you'll want to protect. If you don't have an automated means of backing up your data, such as using Apple's Backup program that is included with a .Mac account, I encourage you to add one more item to your weekly To Do list: Export your iCal calendar.

Go to *File → Export*, and then choose the destination for your backup file. iCal will create an *.ics* file containing all of your important data. I recommend that you keep a copy of this information on a separate hard drive, or even burn it to CD along with your Address Book backup. Either way, regular archiving protects your data in the event that your PowerBook is damaged or lost.

After you start using iCal, you may want to share your calendar with others. This advanced feature enables you to display your calendar on the Internet so others can view your appointments. The easiest way to do this is via a .Mac account. If you want to learn more about publishing your calendars, go to: *www.apple.com/ical*. Apple also maintains an entire calendar library, such as U.S. holidays, sporting events, and movie openings you can subscribe to and receive updates over the Internet. To browse these calendars, click on the Calendar Library button on the iCal web page.

Random notes with Stickies

Now that you've set up Address Book to organize your contacts and iCal to keep track of when you're going to meet them, what do you use to stay on top of the odds and ends in life that are neither contacts, regular To Dos, or appointments? Apple provides you with a "catch all" solution called Stickies.

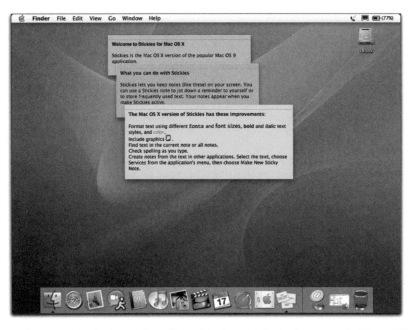

Instead of posting stickies on the refrigerator where you'll eventually lose them, use the digital version on your PowerBook. They won't fall off your screen when you're not looking.

Connecting with
Your PowerBook

Care and
Feeding

Getting
Started

Organize
Your Life

Your Digital
Lifestyle

PowerBook on
the Go

These electronic Post It notes are perfect for jotting short reminders and small bits of temporary information—in much the same way you've most likely come to use them in your daily life. You can find Stickies in your Applications folder and on the Dock.

Working with these notes is an intuitive process. To create a new note, go to *File → New Note*, or type ⌘-N. You're presented with the standard yellow note. You can type your info and be done with it. Or you can customize your notes by adding specific colors. When you've clicked on a note, go to Color on the top menu bar and select a different hue. Conceivably you can organize your notes by using this option. Work notes could be yellow and personal items colored blue.

Stickies Backup

You saw earlier that both Address Book and iCal have backup functionality built right into their respective applications. But Stickies doesn't. In order to ensure that you don't lose your notes in case of failure or loss, find the file *StickiesDatabase* located in your Library folder in your Home directory (*Home → Library → StickiesDatabase*). You can easily copy the file to an external hard drive by drag and drop. You might also want to burn it on the same CD as your backups for Address Book and iCal. If you're a .Mac subscriber, the included Backup application does enable you to automatically archive your Stickies.

When you quit Stickies, the program will save all of the new information you've recently added. You can also manually save by using the Save command: *File → Save All*. If you attempt to close an individual Sticky without saving it, the application will present you with a dialog box asking if you want to keep it. Chances are, the answer will be yes.

You can print just one note, or all of them using the Print commands under the File menu. But the one really handy tool that I want to point out for managing a whole screen full of Stickies is Expose, which we covered in Chapter 2. Remember the *Organize Application Windows* function you set then? This is a handy tool when you have dozens of Stickies posted on your PowerBook. To find the one you need to refer to, hit F10 (if you followed the set up I outlined for Expose) or move the pointer to the upper-left corner of your PowerBook screen.

You'll see all of your Stickies at once! Now just click on the one you want to refer to, and it comes forward and all the others move behind it. If you didn't love Exposé before, I know you will now.

Once again I want to refer you to the Stickies Help menu (at the top of the menu bar) for more information about how to use this handy application. I would avoid keeping information here that is better suited for Address Book and iCal, but for temporary notes, this tool is fun to use and quite effective.

Your PowerBook is becoming more valuable by the hour. You have customized its appearance to your tastes, you're communicating via email, looking things up on the Web, managing your appointments with iCal, keeping track of people with Address Book, and even posting the occasional reminder on your screen with Stickies. What more could your PowerBook possibly do?

Connecting with
Your PowerBook

Care and
Feeding

Getting
Started

Organize
Your Life

Your Digital
Lifestyle

PowerBook on
the Go

That great feeling of organization

Lots more! Next I'll provide you with a few insights on how your PowerBook can help you manage your music collection, digital photos, and even home movies. So take a quick break, and then join me for the next chapter.

Connecting with
Your PowerBook

Care and
Feeding

Getting
Started

Organize
Your Life

Your Digital
Lifestyle

PowerBook on
the Go

By this point, you've done quite a bit of tinkering with your PowerBook. That's to be expected, at least in the beginning.

But you didn't purchase a Mac to make these sort of tasks your life's work. In the bigger picture, computers are designed to help you get things done. For one person, the goal could be using the PowerBook to help manage email and online browsing. For another, the most important function might be organizing a busy life with Address Book and iCal.

More and more, however, the driving force to owning a laptop is to enjoy digital music, photography, and video. If you share any of these interests, then you've selected the right computer. The PowerBook, with its suite of "iApps" built right in, is a magnificent device for pursuing your interests in digital media.

This chapter will help you get started by introducing you to iPhoto, iTunes, and iMovie. Plus I'll show you some great accessories (toys) that will further enhance this experience.

Get the picture with iPhoto

I fondly refer to iPhoto as a digital shoebox. Why's that? Because it harkens back to our old habit of stuffing drugstore envelopes full of prints into shoeboxes, and then sliding them under the bed. This wasn't exactly an elegant storage system, but it did work. That is, until you had to retrieve a specific snapshot. "Egads, which envelope? Which box?" Yes, the drawback to this system is that you can't enjoy your entire photo collection—only those pictures you can actually find.

iPhoto's two-column window lists your master Photo Library and custom albums in the left-side Source pane, and displays your thumbnails in the window on the right. Most of the navigation and function tools are located at the bottom of the window.

Connecting with
Your PowerBook

Care and
Feeding

Getting
Started

Organize
Your Life

Your Digital
Lifestyle

PowerBook on
the Go

Your PowerBook is about to change all that, thanks to a little program called iPhoto. Think of it as your digital shoebox that actually makes it easy to find your pictures. Beyond that, you can adjust, print, and share them with others—all using iPhoto's built-in tools.

Unfortunately, I can't help you with all of those old pictures under the bed. That requires a scanner and lots of rainy days with nothing else to do. But I can help you start anew and stay organized from this day forward. First, you need to transfer the photos from your digital camera to iPhoto. The simplest method is to connect your camera to the computer using the USB cable that came with it in the box. Now turn on the power, and your digicam will start a conversation that goes a little something like this:

> "Hello PowerBook, I'm the digital camera around these parts. I have some pictures for you."

> "Glad to meet you, camera. I'm a computer with a nice big hard drive; I'll take those images off your plate and store them for you. Let me launch iPhoto and we'll be on our way. Okay, I'm ready to go. All I need is for our owner to click on the Import button now showing on the screen."

And that's what you do. You click on the blue Import button in the lower-right corner of the iPhoto window and the pictures move from the camera to your PowerBook.

Where Not to Erase Pictures

Sometimes applications can be too helpful. iPhoto's *Erase camera contents after transfer* (located beneath the Import button) is a great example of an option *not to use.* Leave this box unchecked. If something goes wrong during the picture upload, you don't want iPhoto wiping out your memory card. Plus, your digital camera will do a much better job of erasing pictures off the card than iPhoto.

The second option for upload is to attach a memory card reader to the PowerBook. In this case you take the memory card out of the camera, insert it in the reader, and click on iPhoto's Import button. The advantage of this method is that you don't use any of your camera's battery power to transfer pictures. Plus, the new FireWire (and USB 2.0) readers move data faster than the camera's slower USB (1.1) connection. The only catch? Make sure you buy a reader that accepts the type of memory cards your camera uses.

In some recent tests I conducted, the SanDisk Ultra FireWire ImageMate Reader uploaded images to iPhoto over twice as fast than when I connected a Canon Digital Elph directly to the computer using its USB cable. So there is definitely a speed difference between the two methods. The downside is that you have an extra device to keep track of when you use an external memory card reader.

The Belkin Hi-Speed USB 2.0 15-in-1 Media Reader & Writer lets you download your digital camera images to iPhoto at a blazing 480Mbps— 40 times faster than USB 1.1 readers. Plus it accommodates just about every type of media card (about $50 www.belkin.com).

Connecting with
Your PowerBook

Care and
Feeding

Getting
Started

Organize
Your Life

Your Digital
Lifestyle

PowerBook on
the Go

Regardless of which method you use to upload your pictures, you'll see your iPhoto window fill with thumbnail images. Pick one and double-click it. You're greeted with an enlarged view of the image you double-clicked. You've gone from Organize mode to Edit mode. If you want to return to your thumbnail, just click once on the Organize button in the toolbar directly below the picture. The thumbnails return!

Pick another photo and double-click it taking you back to Edit mode. You'll see that the icons at the bottom of iPhoto's interface change to a set of photo tools. If you want to crop your image, for example, just click and drag your pointer across the area of the picture you want to retain and press the crop button. If you don't like the change, you can undo it by going to *Edit → Undo*, located at the top menu bar.

Revert to Orginal

iPhoto knows that sometimes you make big mistakes when editing your pictures. That's why, no matter what you do to your photographs in Edit mode, you always have the option to revert to the original image you uploaded from your camera. You can find that command on the top menu bar: *Photos → Revert to Original*. Now you have no excuse not to experiment and play with your images, because you always have this safety net beneath you.

PowerBook
Fan Book

You have other tools to play with on the toolbar, but most people find that using Crop and Brightness/Contrast satisfies most of their photo adjustment needs.

Even though you can see thumbnails of all of your pictures when you click on Photo Library in the upper-left corner of iPhoto's window, you may want to create some subcategories to make browsing more efficient, such as building a photo album for a recent vacation, and then creating a different one for this year's graduation ceremonies.

The Lexar CF FireWire Card Reader is as capable as it is compact. It downloads your pictures from CompactFlash Type I & II cards at 400Mbps (about $50 www.lexar.com).

All you have to do is click the "+" button in the lower-left corner of iPhoto's window, and give the new album a name. It will be added to the Source pane below the Photo Library (that's always located at the top of the heap). To add pictures to the new album, click and drag thumbnails into it. Hold down the ⌘ key to select random images at once, or hold down the Shift key as you click on the first and last in a sequence to highlight them all.

When you drag those selected thumbnails into an album, you're not moving them out of the master Photo Library. You're only creating "visual pointers" to the original pictures.

That also means that you can delete photos out of your custom albums, and they will still reside in your master Photo Library. But if you delete an image out of the Photo Library itself, it's gone.

Good digital photos begin with good digital cameras. The Canon PowerShot Digital Elph S500 is a compact "take anywhere" 5-megapixel digicam that works smoothly with iPhoto (about $450 www.powershot.com).

Connecting with
Your PowerBook

Care and
Feeding

Getting
Started

Organize
Your Life

**Your Digital
Lifestyle**

PowerBook on
the Go

After you've moved pictures to a custom album, click on it to see what you've created. One fun thing to do (when you've clicked on and highlighted a custom album) is to click on the Slideshow button in the lower-left corner of the iPhoto window. You'll be asked to make a few quick choices, such as selecting your preferred type of transition and how long each image stays on the screen, then click the Play button. You now get to enjoy a full screen slideshow of the pictures in that album. Try to do that with drugstore prints!

Other buttons at the bottom of the iPhoto window enable you to email pictures, set your Desktop background (wallpaper), print from your inkjet printer, and order prints online. You can learn more about these capabilities by visiting Apple's iPhoto web page: *www.apple.com/ilife/iphoto/.* Also, iPhoto's Help menu is chock-full of practical tips and techniques. Be sure to check it out.

And if you really want to learn the ins and outs of this cool application, then don't forget the definitive guide—*iPhoto 4: The Missing Manual,* by David Pogue and yours truly. You can order it online from *www.oreilly.com.*

The Epson R200 ($99) and R300 ($179) inkjet printers are great buys in 6-color photo printing. Both provide BorderFree printing at sizes up to 8" x 10". The R300 includes built-in memory card slots for nearly every type of digital camera media (*www.epson.com*).

Before I move on to digital music, I want to cover one very important technique that will help you have a long, prosperous digital photography experience: back up your pictures. Sooner or later, every hard drive in every computer will crash. If that ever happens to you, don't let all of your valuable images go down with it. Preserve them on optical media, and iPhoto makes that process easy.

Depending on how much you shoot, back up every few weeks, or at least once a month. First, go to the Source pane where all of your custom albums reside. Hold down the ⌘ key and highlight (by clicking once on them) the albums you've created since the last backup. Then click on the Burn button in the lower-right corner of iPhoto. You'll be asked to insert a blank CD. Once iPhoto has approved of the blank CD, it will tell you how much of it is being used for this backup in the information area above the Comments field. You can also add a custom name for your CD here if you want. I recommend that you do.

Click the Burn button again and iPhoto will write those albums to CD. After the burn is completed, write descriptive information on the outside of the CD so it's easy to identify in the future. My guess is that you'll accumulate lots of CDs over the years. Make sure you can sort through them easily. If you need to see the actual pictures on a particular backup CD, just insert it in your drive and iPhoto will add it to your list of albums. You can browse the archived images just like any other custom album.

Lowepro Digital Wallet (D Res 4) and SanDisk Ultra Memory Cards. The Lowepro wallet ($10, *www.lowepro.com*) is the perfect home to protect spare memory cards and your PC Card reader. SanDisk Ultra II memory cards are rugged and have a minimum write speed of 9MB per second with low power consumption (*www.sandisk.com*). SanDisk prices vary according to type of memory and capacity.

Connecting with
Your PowerBook

Care and
Feeding

Getting
Started

Organize
Your Life

**Your Digital
Lifestyle**

PowerBook on
the Go

The beauty of this system is that you don't have to copy the pictures off the CD to your hard drive to enjoy them. iPhoto lets you make prints and build slideshows directly off the optical media. Over time, this helps you manage space on your PowerBook's hard drive while still keeping all of your photos accessible.

To make sure you don't forget to back up your pictures, go to iCal right now and create a repeating event that displays every month in your calendar. That way, you have no excuse.

Upload your next batch of digital pictures to iPhoto and give it a try. Explore all of its features. My guess is that you'll never go back to stashing photos under the bed in old shoeboxes.

PowerBook
Fan Book

The joy of digital music

Digital music has become synonymous with Apple's iTunes and iPod. And for good reason. This powerful combination enables you to acquire and manage music on a Mac, and take it anywhere you go with an iPod. And it all works together in perfect harmony.

Similar to iPhoto, iTune's two-column window lists your master music Library and custom albums in the left-side Source pane, and displays your songs in the window on the right. Navigation and function tools are located at both the top and the bottom of the window. You'll even get a picture of the album cover if you bought the song from the iTunes Music Store.

Connecting with
Your PowerBook

Care and
Feeding

Getting
Started

Organize
Your Life

**Your Digital
Lifestyle**

PowerBook on
the Go

Even if you don't own an iPod, you can enjoy the digital music experience. Your PowerBook is the perfect device for organizing your existing library of CDs, acquiring new songs through the iTunes Music Store, and listening to your collection via headphones or piped through external speakers.

The best place to start is with the music you already own. Chances are you have many great songs tucked away on CDs that are lost deep in the recesses of your home entertainment system. Start by digging through those albums and selecting a dozen that will serve as the foundation of your digital music collection.

Set up your work area in a visible part of the room so you can see the PowerBook screen while you multitask during the *ripping* process—that is, transferring the contents of your CDs to the computer's hard drive. This takes a few minutes for each disc, so you might want to do other tasks at the same time, such as dig through the home entertainment center for more CDs. Believe me, ripping music becomes an addictive activity.

PowerBook
Fan Book

The Sony SRS-T88 powered speakers pack big sound into a small package. Total power output of 4Ws provides plenty of boost for your iTunes music. World voltage adapter (100V–240V) saves battery power when outlets are available (about $89 www.sony.com).

You'll also need an Internet connection. Why? All the valuable album information for each CD you own is stored in an Internet database that iTunes will check, then actually grab that data so you don't have to type it in. This is very important because it saves you the tedious labor of having to enter by hand the album name, artist, and each song title. You'll fall in love with this free service. It's called the CDDB—"Compact Disc Database."

After you have your first batch of CDs selected, your work area set up, and PowerBook connected to the Internet, launch iTunes, which is located in your Applications folder and on the Dock. The interface should feel familiar by now, because Apple is consistent in how it designs its software. In the left column, you'll see a few icons. The most important ones to note right now are Library and Music Store. Library is similar to Photo Library in iPhoto, meaning that when you click on it, every song you have stored in iTunes appears in the right column. And just like iPhoto, you can create custom albums by clicking on the "+" icon in the lower-left corner, and then drag songs from the Library to your custom album. Remember, you're not actually moving the songs out of the master library, just creating pointers to them (the same as in iPhoto).

The Music Store icon takes you, appropriately enough, to Apple's online music store. Here you can buy individual songs, ad hoc playlists and collections, and whole albums— all downloaded directly to your iTunes library for you. I'm not going to spend time in the store right now because you have to pay for that music. Instead, let's work with the stuff you already own.

To make sure you import your music properly, I want you to open iTunes Preferences and check a few settings (*iTunes → Preferences*). Refer to the table below and make sure your settings match those I've listed there.

Icon	Setting
General	Check the box labeled *Connect to Internet when needed*
Importing	Import Using: MP3 Encoder; Setting: High Quality (160 kbps)
	Check the box labeled *Create file names with track number*
	Check box labeled *Play songs while importing* (optional)
Advanced	Check the box labeled *Keep iTunes Music folder organized*
	Check the box labeled *Copy files to iTunes Music folder*

Connecting with
Your PowerBook

Care and
Feeding

Getting
Started

Organize
Your Life

Your Digital
Lifestyle

PowerBook on
the Go

Serious music aficionados might debate these choices, especially the selected encoder under Importing. I recommend that you use MP3 over other options (including Apple's favorite, AAC) because MP3 is still the most versatile format. You can share songs encoded as MP3s with just about anyone and play them on virtually any digital music device, as well as PDAs and some smartphones. If you have preferences for another format, by all means use it. But if you're just starting out, this is a good way to go.

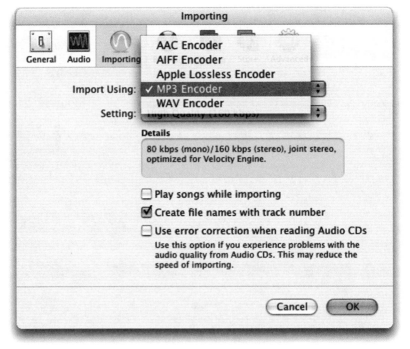

You have lots of encoder options, but MP3 is still the most versatile format for ripping your CDs.

Click OK to save your preferences, and you're now ready to rip your first CD. This is the fun part! Insert the music disc into your PowerBook. After a few seconds (but it seems longer than it should be) the CD icon will appear on your desktop, and iTunes will query the CDDB naming service. This is why you need to be connected to the Internet. Within a short time iTunes will have retrieved the information it needs, and the music data magically appears in the main window. You have just saved yourself lots of typing.

So what happens if you don't use this service? Your songs will still import, but they'll be listed in iTunes as Track 1, Track 2, and so forth. You'll have no idea what the song title is, and after importing hundreds of tunes, you can see the problem this presents. Avoid the whole mess by using the free CDDB service. As I mentioned earlier, it is a godsend.

When you want to enjoy your digital music collection, but don't want to bring your PowerBook, the iPod is the perfect music jukebox for on the go (starting at $249 www.apple.com/itunes).

Connecting with
Your PowerBook

Care and
Feeding

Getting
Started

Organize
Your Life

**Your Digital
Lifestyle**

PowerBook on
the Go

You'll also notice that the CD icon has been added to the left Source column in iTunes a little ways below the Library icon and all of the songs from that CD are listed in the main window with checked boxes next to them. If there's a song you don't want to rip, just uncheck the box and iTunes will bypass it. In the upper-right corner of the iTunes window, the Browse button has become the Import button. Click this to initiate the transfer of music from the audio CD to iTunes.

iTunes goes to work importing your music. It will also play songs while doing so if you've set that option under the Importing category in Preferences. After a song has been transferred to the hard drive, it will have a green check mark next to it. The orange squiggle indicates which song is currently being ripped.

I'm always impressed at how fast iTunes encodes the music. An entire album only takes a few minutes. There's no need to sit there and watch this process, but don't wander too far away if you want to keep the process moving along. iTunes will be finished before you know it and waiting for the next CD to rip.

PowerBook
Fan Book

Sennheiser PX 100 are simply some of the best portable headphones I've listened to. Their fold-and-flip design, complete with hard plastic case, help them fit in the tightest of laptop bags. The sound is balanced and rich with plenty of bass (about $39 *www.sennheiser.com*).

After all the songs have been transferred, you should create a custom album for them. Click on the "+" button in the lower-left corner to create your new album, and then type in the name. Now click on the Library icon at the top of the source window. You'll see the new songs you've just imported. Click once on the top one, hold down the Shift key, and click once on the last song—they will all be highlighted. Drag the songs to your new custom album. You've done it! You can double-check your success by clicking once on the custom album name to reveal all of the songs, then double-click any of the selections to begin playback.

Griffin PowerWave USB audio interface and amplifier is called the "Swiss Army knife for sound." And for good reason. The 10-watt per channel amplifier enables you to connect just about any audio device into your Mac or output from your PowerBook. Perfect for digitizing old cassette tapes and vinyl albums (about $100 www.griffintechnology.com).

Connecting with
Your PowerBook

Care and
Feeding

Getting
Started

Organize
Your Life

Your Digital
Lifestyle

PowerBook on
the Go

You can change the order within this playlist by clicking and dragging the songs to their new position. If you want to review the data associated with a song, click on it once to highlight it, and then go to *File → Get Info*. Here, you can see all of the encoding information under the Summary button. If you want to add your own comments, click on the Info button right next to Summary, and type in any of the fields. Click OK when you're finished.

Now you're ready to rip the next CD. Go to *Controls → Eject CD* (on the top menu bar) to remove the disc that you just encoded, insert the next one and start all over again.

Smart Playlists Create Element of Surprise

After you've imported your first batch of CDs, you might want to listen to your music in a new and creative way. Instead of playing the same old songs you always play, why not let iTunes put together a playlist for you that plays tunes you haven't listened to lately?

Select *File → New Smart Playlist*. You'll be presented with a dialog box. Choose *Last Played* from the left drop-down menu and then select *Is not in the last* from the next menu. Put the number 2 in the open field, then select Weeks from the far right drop-down menu. Check the box labeled *Limit to* and leave 25 as the number of songs. Click OK. iTunes will create a new Smart Playlist and add it to the Source window. All you have to do now is name it something like "Buried Treasures." That playlist will constantly change depending on the music you listen to in your library.

As your iTunes library grows, you might have a hard time finding a particular song, or collection of songs that you've just imported. Your library list is going to get pretty long. Instead of browsing the list trying to find the song you want, enter the song name or artist in the Search window (in the upper-right hand corner), and that song or group of songs will appear in the main window. Much easier, isn't it?

This is only the beginning of what you can do with iTunes and your digital music collection. You can purchase songs by clicking on the Music Store icon (when connected to the Internet). You can also burn CDs with your personal playlists, and you can even share music with others over a wireless network (called streaming music).

Visit Apple's web page at *http://www.apple.com/itunes* for more information. One of my favorite books on this subject is *iPod & iTunes: The Missing Manual* by J.D. Biersdorfer *(www.oreilly.com/catalog/ipodtmm2)*. And don't forget to browse Help (on the menu bar) for more details about getting the most from your digital music experience.

Connecting with
Your PowerBook

Care and
Feeding

Getting
Started

Organize
Your Life

Your Digital
Lifestyle

PowerBook on
the Go

Transform dull video into exciting iMovies

Watching digital video usually means connecting your camcorder to your television set and hitting the play button. No titles, transitions, and certainly (read: unfortunately) no editing. If you happen to be the unlucky person to whom the movie is being shown, you're at least hoping that the presenter is also familiar with the fast forward button. Otherwise, you're likely to be in for a long night.

iMovie stores your video clips on the right side in the Clips Pane. You can preview your work in the large Monitor Pane on the left. The Scrubber Bar is right below the Monitor and the Playhead is positioned to the far left. During playback, the Playhead moves to the right indicating where you are in the clip. Below the Scrubber Bar are the playback controls. At the bottom of the window is the Clip Viewer, where you position your snippets in the order you want them to play in your final movie.

The good news is that iMovie can rescue you from amateur video hell. This handy video editing application enables you to extract the interesting moments from your video, stitch them together, and then save them back to a fresh DV tape for playback on a TV or video monitor. This simple process is priceless for family and friends who would much rather watch an engaging 4-minute movie of your daughter's second birthday party than the entire event in real time.

To create your masterpiece, all you need is your PowerBook, iMovie (which you can find in the Applications folder), a 6-pin to 4-pin FireWire cable for transfer, and your DV camcorder. I also think it's a good idea to connect your camcorder to an external power source while editing so you don't run out of power.

When you launch iMovie for the first time, it will ask you if you want to create a new project. You do, so click the *Create new project* button. You're now presented with the iMovie work area. The video clips are stored on the right side of the window called the Clip Pane. The big screen is called the iMovie monitor—it's where you watch preview clips and finished movies. The rectangular box that runs along the bottom is called the Clip Viewer, and that's where you position your clips in the order you want the movie to flow.

Apple's iSight webcam enables you to record audio and video in iMovie. Griffin Technology's SightLight makes your movies look even better. The SightLight shares the iSight's FireWire cable to put you in a better light (about $40 *www.griffintechnology.com*).

Connecting with
Your PowerBook

Care and
Feeding

Getting
Started

Organize
Your Life

Your Digital
Lifestyle

PowerBook on
the Go

Before you connect the camera, go to Preferences (*iMovie → Preferences*) and check the box labeled *Automatically start new clip at scene break*. This single act will make your world a better place. Instead of creating one long unmanageable video stream during upload, iMovie will sense the scene breaks and create a series of manageable video clips for you to work with.

Now connect your DV camcorder via the FireWire cable (old style VHS camcorders won't work with iMovie, you need a modern DV model), and turn it on to playback mode. If everything is connected correctly, iMovie's monitor screen will change from black to a pretty blue and will state, "Camera Connected." You're now ready to go to work.

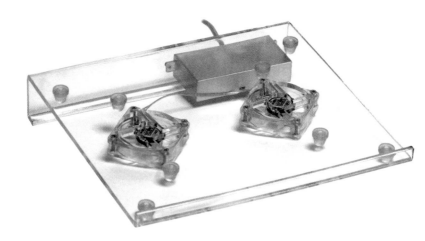

Video editing is processor-intensive work, and your PowerBook might get a little warm during long stretches. The iBreeze laptop stand has two built-in fans that will keep your PowerBook cool and happy. And the best part is that the fans are powered from one of the PowerBook's two USB ports (about $30 *www.macmice.com*).

You can use iMovie's playback controls to operate your DV camcorder, which is a great convenience. Press the big triangle button in the center of iMovie's toolbar, for example, and your PowerBook will instruct the DV camcorder to start playing the tape. You can watch it in iMovie's monitor pane. Hit the squarish Stop button and playback stops.

To start importing video, click on the Import button above the Pay button, and iMovie saves the video that you see playing on the monitor to the PowerBook's hard disk. Click the Import button again to stop uploading. If you do nothing but hit the Import button and leave it on during playback, iMovie will create a new clip automatically at every scene break. Or you can control this process manually by clicking the Import button on and off during play. In video terminology, this method is called "capture on the fly."

You'll begin to pile up a bunch of snippets in the clips pane. I don't recommend that you upload hours of video at first because this content takes a tremendous amount of hard disc space—one gigabyte of disk space for every four and a half minutes of video. You can monitor the free space remaining on your hard drive by checking the status indicator in the lower-right corner of iMovie's window.

After you capture the video you need, it's time to trim your clips to eliminate the unnecessary footage. Click once on your first clip to present it on the monitor. iMovie will automatically switch modes from camera mode to edit mode (as represented by the scissors icon).

Move your trackpad pointer to the blue scrubber bar that sits at the bottom of the monitor pane. You'll see two little triangles appear on the left end of the scrubber bar. Drag these pointers to select the endpoints of the video segment you want to keep—that segment will turn yellow on the scrubber bar (see illustration). Choose *Edit → Crop* at the top menu bar, and iMovie will discard all the content on the outside of the pointers. You've now cropped your video. If you didn't get it just right, you can always choose *Edit → Undo* and iMovie will restore the entire clip to its original state.

Connecting with
Your PowerBook

Care and
Feeding

Getting
Started

Organize
Your Life

**Your Digital
Lifestyle**

PowerBook on
the Go

One of iMovie's most powerful
features is enabling you to
crop your video clips. In editing
mode (notice the scissors icon
is selected), drag the bottom
triangles on the scrubber bar
to select the endpoints of the
segment you want to keep
(indicated by yellow). Then go
to *Edit → Crop* to trim away
the excess footage (indicated
by blue).

PowerBook
Fan Book

Repeat this cropping process with all of segments in the clips pane. You can also copy and paste selected areas when simple cropping might not work well. After you've edited each clip, you're ready to begin building your movie. Drag the clips one by one down to the clips viewer. Put them in the order you want. If you want to change the order, drag them to their new location.

You can preview your movie by clicking on the small triangle in the black rectangle, and iMovie will play your new creation on the full screen. If the movie isn't starting at the beginning, click on the double-triangles to the left of the playback button. They will relocate the Playhead to the far left of the scrubber bar—the beginning of your movie.

Before you export your movie back to DV tape, you can add titles, transitions, and even background music. Refer to iMovie's excellent Help menu for more information about these features.

To finish this process, turn off your camcorder and put a fresh tape in it. This will be your "showcase" tape with all of your finished movies. Turn the camcorder back on and wait for the blue screen to appear again in the monitor window.

Go to *iMovie → Share* on the top menu bar, and click on the Video Camera icon. You can adjust the default settings, such as telling iMovie how many seconds of black you want before the movie starts playing, or just leave them as is. Then click the Share button. iMovie will write your edited video back to the camcorder—complete with edits, titles, and anything else you used to enhance your piece.

LaCie's popular D2 series of external hard drives are excellent for backing up large iMovie files. I recommend the 250 GB model (about $280 www.lacie.com).

Connecting with
Your PowerBook

Care and
Feeding

Getting
Started

Organize
Your Life

Your Digital
Lifestyle

PowerBook on
the Go

Now you can connect your camcorder to a television and share your finished product with others. iMovie also lets you export movies to Web pages, DVD discs, or as email attachments and standalone QuickTime movies. It can even send theses pieces to Bluetooth-enabled smartphones capable of playing digital media.

See the Help menu to learn more about your sharing options. And don't forget to save your project regularly (*File → Save Project*). Also, keep in mind that your project folder is stored in the Movies folder in your Home directory.

After you finish working on a movie, I recommend that you copy this folder to DVD (on SuperDrive capable PowerBooks) or to an external FireWire drive. That way, you are free to remove the voluminous project folder, thereby freeing up gigabytes of disk space on your PowerBook.

To work on the movie again, just copy the project folder back to your Movies folder, launch iMovie, and direct the movie to the project folder. All of your clips will appear just as you had left them.

By applying just these few simple techniques to your captured digital video, your movies will rise head and shoulders above those who choose not to edit, most likely because they don't have a Mac.

For more information, be sure to visit Apple's iMovie web page at *www.apple.com/ilife/imovie/* for many great tips for importing, editing, adding audio effects, and sharing your completed masterpieces with others.

I also highly recommend *iMovie 4 & iDVD: The Missing Manual* by David Pogue and available from O'Reilly Media (*www.oreilly.com/catalog/imoviemm4/index.html*) for $25.

Monster iTV Link for 15" and 17" Power Books. Show your iMovies (or DVDs) on the big screen with the iTV Link. Quality construction delivers the best picture possible from your PowerBook to the television (about $40 *www.monstercable.com*).

Are you feeling digital?

I've just covered the very basics of digital photography, music, and video on the PowerBook. You have hours of exploration ahead of you. As you become proficient with these basic digital media applications, you can move on to more sophisticated programs such as GarageBand and iDVD.

Apple provides you with just about every tool you'll need. All you have to add is a little creativity.

PowerBook on the Go 5

Connecting with
Your PowerBook

Care and
Feeding

Getting
Started

Organize
Your Life

Your Digital
Lifestyle

PowerBook on
the Go

The PowerBook is freedom. Your productivity is no longer chained to a desk or trapped in a cubicle. All you need is a place to sit, a charged battery, and your Mac. The first time you open its brushed aluminum case in a park, at a coffee shop, or even on the patio outside your backdoor, you'll experience the wave of euphoria that comes with untethered computing.

The built-in AirPort wireless networking gives you even more sovereignty. With it, you can send and receive email while sipping an espresso at the local corner coffee bar (instead of that brown colored water they offer at work). You can shop online while enjoying a summer morning on the front porch. Heck, there isn't really anything you can't do if there's a network within reach.

In this chapter I'll introduce some of my favorite PowerBook accessories that let you to enjoy the comforts of home, even though you're miles away from your desk. Some of these items may already be familiar to you. But I guarantee that you'll discover a surprise or two that you'll want to add to your bag of tricks.

PowerBook
Fan Book

Between you and your PowerBook

Yes, we refer to PowerBooks as laptops. But unless you're wearing asbestos-lined pants, these guys soon feel more like hotplates than computers. LapLogic comes to our rescue with a modern-day potholder called the LapPad. This lightweight shield goes between the PowerBook and your lap, protecting you from the heat the computer generates. The stylish LapPad features non-slip surfaces on the outside covering magical metallic insulating fabrics on the inside.

The Chinook T550 is the top-of-the-line model and intercepts up to 54 degrees of heat. The LapLogic pad fits easily in backpacks and cases. It's also handy for protecting delicate wood surfaces from being marred by constant heat output or your PowerBook's little rubber feet. And even though it doesn't say so in the documentation, you can also use the LapLogic pad to sit comfortably on glaciers and other icy surfaces. Hey, you never know. As I said earlier, the PowerBook is born to run.

Your lap stays cool even when your PowerBook heats up when you put the LapLogic Chinook in between (about $45 www.laplogic.com).

Connecting with
Your PowerBook

Care and
Feeding

Getting
Started

Organize
Your Life

Your Digital
Lifestyle

PowerBook on
the Go

If you want to have the option to work at a desk as well as on your lap, I recommend the iLap available from Rain Design. The silver anodized aluminum with cushy velvet wrist rest looks fabulous with the PowerBooks while keeping you comfortable while working.

The front velvet cushion can be removed for desk work, but is very nice when you have your PowerBook on your lap. The iLap is a luxury that you might not take on the plane because it is bulkier than other solutions such as the LapLogic, but when traveling by car or setting up shop away from home, you'll be thrilled to have it with you.

The iLap comes in 12", 15", and 17" sizes to match your PowerBook. The front pad is detachable and the back base swivels (about $60 *www. raindesigninc.com*).

Uniquely USB

Your PowerBook has not one, but two USB ports. So you'd think that they must be there for a reason—and indeed they are. Printers, keyboards, digital cameras, scanners, mice, and even high-tech knobs use this connection.

Griffin Technology has devised one of the most creative of these USB devices—the PowerMate. This high-quality machined aluminum knob is really an assignable controller that you can program (with included software) to adjust volume, edit movies, or scroll through long documents and Web pages. Its compact design is perfect for the digital media professional on the go.

The Griffin Technology PowerMate USB multimedia controller and input device looks and feels like a knob pulled off the front of a world-class stereo. But it's fully programmable and looks great with your PowerBook (about $40 *www.griffintechnology.com*).

Connecting with
Your PowerBook

Care and
Feeding

Getting
Started

Organize
Your Life

Your Digital
Lifestyle

PowerBook on
the Go

For more intense expeditions, urban commandos will appreciate this connectivity travel kit made by Zip-Linq. The Road Warrior package includes four innovative Zip-Linq retractable cables, a two-button mouse with scroll wheel, and a flexible USB-powered light for working discreetly in darkened environments—including your hotel room after the lights have gone out and your bunkmate is trying to sleep.

Zip-Linq cables extend and retract from a tiny center hub. They are quite compact and well made. The Road Warrior kit includes connectors for your PowerBook's USB ports, plus cables for modem and Ethernet. The mouse works great without any additional drivers, although I recommend that you adjust its tracking speed in the Keyboard & Mouse System Preference pane. (See Chapter 2 for more information.)

The USB light is a white LED powered solely by a single USB port. It's fully adjustable via the 17" arm made out of black PVC-jacketed flexible steel. You can angle it to shine on the keyboard in darkened rooms or to shed a little extra light on paper documents that you're referring to while working.

You can pack the entire Road Warrior Kit inside the included nylon bag with its locking drawstring. No serious metropolitan explorer should leave home without it.

The Zip-Linq Road Warrior kit includes four
innovative retractable cables, an optical USB
mouse, and a flexible LED light (about $60 www.
ziplinq.com).

And what do you do if you end up with more USB devices than ports to plug them in to? Take a look at the Iogear USB 2.0 Microhub. Micro is the operative word here. This device is extremely compact and light, yet it enables you to convert one USB port into four. It's USB 2.0 compatible, so you don't compromise any speed when connecting your latest devices.

My favorite feature is the USB connecting plug that is cleverly hidden on the underside and pops out when needed. You don't have to pack any extra connectors what so ever. The Iogear hub is clever, handsome, and works great.

The Iogear USB 2.0 Microhub is as handsome as it is effective. And it's so light you'll barely feel it in your top shirt pocket (about $40 *www.iogear.com*).

Connecting with
Your PowerBook

Care and
Feeding

Getting
Started

Organize
Your Life

Your Digital
Lifestyle

PowerBook on
the Go

Wireless wonders

Apple's PowerBooks include integrated wireless networking called AirPort.

AirPort-enabled PowerBooks can connect to the Internet anywhere there's an 802.11 wireless network. And these days, there are quite a few places, including coffee shops, airports, hotels, and even many McDonald's restaurants *(www.mcdwireless.com)*.

Apple's AirPort Express Base Station extends this capability to your home, classroom, office, or anywhere that has broadband Internet access. This handy device looks like the power adapter that comes with your PowerBook, but a tad bigger. There are three ports on the bottom. The first is for an Ethernet connection enabling you to plug in the wire from your DSL or cable modem (also available in most hotels these days) and share Internet access with up to ten friends within 150 feet (according to spec). Each person needs a wireless card in his computer to complete the connection.

PowerBook
Fan Book

92

Even though it's small enough to fit in your back pocket, Apple's AirPort Express Base Station allows you to share Internet, printing, and even music with up to ten friends within a 150-foot radius (about $129 *www.apple.com*).

The AirPort Express also has a USB port for connecting your inkjet printer. So not only can you share the Internet, but access to your printer as well! You'll also notice that there's a Line Out port enabling you to connect your stereo or powered speakers to the Express. Why would you want to do that? Remember all that music you ripped and organized in iTunes back in Chapter 4? Well now you can stream those songs over the network via AirPort Express to your stereo. Nifty.

If I've piqued your interest with this innovative device, then you might want to take a look at Apple's web page: *www.apple.com/airportexpress* for more information.

AirPort Express is terrific when you want to create your own wireless network, but what if you want to use someone else's? How do you find all of those networks out there in the world? You could walk around with your PowerBook open and AirPort turned on, but that seems a little risky in a bustling city.

One of the items I carry on my keychain is Marware's WiFi Spy. With it you can detect commercial wireless hotspots (such as those at Starbucks coffee shops), home AirPort Base Stations, office wireless access points, and any other 802.11b/g network. All you have to do is press the button on the WiFi Spy and note the LED readout. Four lights indicate a strong network presence, all the way down to one light that tells you the signal isn't very robust from that location.

Once you locate a wireless network, you can fire up your PowerBook and connect. In commercial venues, such as Starbucks coffee shops, there's usually a usage fee that you can pay with a credit card. The going rate is about $6 an hour. At most schools, conferences, and private locations, you only need the permission of the administrator.

Finding a wireless network is as simple as pulling out your car keys if you have the WiFi Spy attached to the ring (about $30 *www.marware.com*).

Connecting with
Your PowerBook

Care and
Feeding

Getting
Started

Organize
Your Life

Your Digital
Lifestyle

PowerBook on
the Go

And if you're having trouble receiving a strong enough signal with your 12" PowerBook, take a look at Quickertek's whip antenna. It can increase signal strength by as much as 50 percent and line-of-sight distance up to 250 yards.

The Quickertek 12" PowerBook whip antenna (they have 15" and 17" models too) adds 5dbi to your wireless reception. But you have to do a little work for the installation—it isn't plug and play (about $90 *www.quickertek.com*).

Extend your PowerBook's memory

Over time you'll accumulate quite a bit of information on your PowerBook's hard drive. Sharing this data among other computers isn't always as easy as it should be. That is, unless you get your hands on one of these two accessories.

I am hooked on pocketable Flash memory drives. In Chapter 3, I introduced you to the Swiss Memory USB that includes 64MBs of memory squeezed in among scissors, a knife, and a screwdriver. But you can also get standalone keychain Flash drives. The first one I want to mention is the Cruzer Titanium by SanDisk. This stylish, rugged, and very fast Flash drive has a whopping 512MB capacity. And it's much faster to mount and copy than most USB Flash drives.

The Cruzer Titanium is a fast high-capacity Flash drive that looks great with your Powerbook (about $150 www.sandisk.com).

If you need less capacity, you can save yourself some money with the Crucial Gizmo, 256MBs of storage in a keychain sized Flash Drive.

The Crucial Gizmo is smaller than a pack of gum, but holds up to 256MBs of data (about $49 www.crucial.com).

Connecting with
Your PowerBook

Care and
Feeding

Getting
Started

Organize
Your Life

Your Digital
Lifestyle

PowerBook on
the Go

For more capacity, don't forget about Apple's superb portable music jukebox, the iPod. Even though it's a bit pricier than a Flash drive, the large-capacity iPods (the white ones, not the colored Minis) can store huge amounts of data. For most people, the entire contents of their PowerBook hard drive can fit on an iPod. Mac users transfer data via the speedy FireWire port. And best of all, tapping this added feature of the iPod doesn't interfere with its ability to play music.

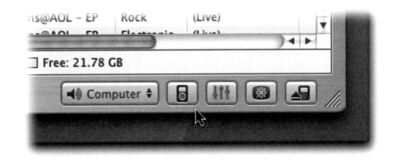

To use the iPod as an external hard drive, connect it to your PowerBook and click on the iPod icon in iTunes.

The trick to setting up your iPod as an external hard drive starts with launching iTunes and clicking on the iPod options button that appears in the lower-right corner (when the iPod is connected). That reveals a preference menu. Check the *Enable disk use* box, and then click OK. Within seconds, your iPod will appear on your PowerBook's desktop. Double-clicking on it reveals a standard Mac OS X window where you can create folders and drag and drop files. When you're finished, just drag the iPod icon to the trash, and then unplug it from your PowerBook.

The white iPods come in 20GB and 40GB models, with 60GB versions just around the corner (they might even be out now). I think they are one of the most exciting portable backup drive solutions because they can do so many handy things. iPods are much more than simple music players.

And for the serious road warrior . . .

I have two more fun accessories that are very handy if you travel with your PowerBook. You could say we're going to wrap up this chapter by powering up and locking down.

Even though your PowerBook battery runs for hours, sometimes that's still not enough. If you're in the car or lucky enough to have an Empower-equipped airline seat (otherwise known as a power plug in the armrest), you can use Kensington's Universal Car/Air Adapter (Model #33051 is for Apple computers) to keep on working. This compact recharger has internal circuitry that protects your notebook and prevents overheating.

The Kensington Car/Air Adapter (#33051) is the perfect solution for recharging on the go when a regular outlet isn't available (about $80 www.kensington.com).

Connecting with
Your PowerBook

Care and
Feeding

Getting
Started

Organize
Your Life

Your Digital
Lifestyle

PowerBook on
the Go

And to protect your investment when staying in hotel rooms and shared work areas, take a look at the Kensington MicroSaver Retractable lock that attaches to the security slot on your PowerBook. The 4-foot rubber coated cable retracts into a compact case that slips easily into your laptop bag.

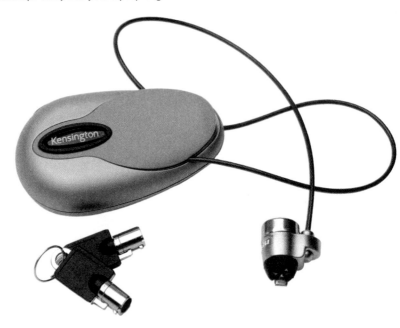

PowerBook
Fan Book

The Kensington MicroSaver retractable security lock protects your PowerBook in hotels and shared work areas (about $30 www.microsaver.com).

Final stop

Now for the hard part—how do you choose which accessory to try first? That probably depends on your particular tastes, and of course, your budget. I hope this guide has demonstrated how much fun PowerBook computing can be. And certainly by now, you've transformed Apple's PowerBook into *your PowerBook.* As they say in the movies, this could be the start of a beautiful friendship.

Index

Symbols

10/100 Ethernet jack (RJ-45), xv

A

AAC format, 70
accessibility, 27
Accounts preference pane, 24–26
    Login Options, 24
    Password pane, 25
    Picture preference pane, 25
    Verify pane, 25
AC power jack, xiv
Address Book, 43–46
    "+" button, 44
    Back Up Database, 45
    Bluetooth-enabled devices, 45
    deleting entries, 44
    Exposé preference pane and, 16
    Group column, 44
    importing data from other organizers, 44
    Make This My Card, 45
    Name column, 44
    populating, 45
    Revert to Database Backup, 46
AIM screen name, 38
AirPort Express Base Station, 92
American Online subscribers, 30
Appearance preference pane, 14
Apple icon, 13
Apple key, xx
arrow keys, xix

B

backing up
    Address Book, 45
    iCal, 52
    images, 65
    Stickies, 54
backpacks, 3–6
Backup program, 52
Back Office backpack, 4
battery power, configuring settings, 19
Belkin Hi-Speed USB 2.0 15-in-1 Media
            Reader & Writer, 61
Bluetooth-enabled devices, 45
bookmarks in Safari, 32
booting the system, xii
browsers, 33
    (see also Safari browser)

C

Cancel, xii
Canon PowerShot Digital Elph S500, 63
cases, 3–6
CDDB (Compact Disc Database), 69, 71
CDs
    burning in iPhoto, 65
    CDs & DVDs preference pane, 18
    inserting, xiii
    ripping, 68, 71
CDs & DVDs preference pane, 18
cleaners, 9
Clock preference pane, 26

Combo drive, xiii
Command key, xx
Crucial Gizmo, 95
Cruzer Titanium, 95
Ctrl key, xx

D

Date & Time preference pane, 26
Desktop & Screensaver preference pane, 14
digital camera memory cards, inserting
    directly, xv
digital music, 67–75
Digital Video (DV) output, xv
Displays preference pane, 18
Dock preference pane, 15
    magnification box, 15
    Minimize function to Scale Effect, 15
DVDs
    CDs & DVDs preference pane, 18
    copying movies to, 82
    inserting, xiii
DV camcorder, 77–79

E

Eject button, xiii
Eject CD command, 74
email (see Mail)
Energy Saver preference pane, 18
    Schedule and Options panes, 19
Entourage, 35, 48
Exposé preference pane, 16
    Address Book and, 16
Exposé web page, 17

F

faxes, Print & Fax preference pane, 20
Firefox, 33
FireWire 400, xv
FireWire 800, xvi
Flash memory drives, 95
function keys, xvii

G

Gigabit Ethernet, xv
Griffin Technology
    PowerMate USB multimedia controller
        and input device, 89
    PowerWave USB audio interface and
        amplifier, 73

H

headphones, 68, 72

I

iBreeze laptop stand, 78
iCal, 47–52
    backing up, 52
    Export, 52
    getting started, 49
    Help menu, 52
    importing data, 48
    Month view, 50
    on Dock, 51
    Preferences, 51
    Search, 52
    synchronizing, 52
    To Do list, 51

iChat, 38–40
  AV web page, 39
  Buddy List window, 38
iKlear Cleaning kit, 9
iMovie, 76–82
  Clip Pane, 77
  Clip Viewer, 77
  Create new project button, 77
  Crop, 79
  exporting movies, 82
  Help menu, 81
  items needed to create video, 77
  monitor, 77
  playback controls, 79
  Preferences, 78
  previewing movie, 80
  Save Project, 82
  scrubber bar, 79
  Share button, 81
  Video Camera icon, 81
instant messaging (IM), 38
International preference pane, 17
Internet applications, 29–40
Internet Connect, 29–30
  American Online subscribers, 30
Internet connections, sharing, 24
Iogear USB 2.0 Microhub, 91
iPhoto, 59–66
  "+" button, 63
  backing up images, 65
  burning CDs, 65
  dragging selected thumbnails into an
    album, 63

Erase camera contents after transfer
    option, 60
Import button, 60
memory card reader, 61
moving photos into album, 63
Revert to Original, 62
Slideshow button, 64
Source pane, 63
switching from Organize mode to Edit
    mode, 62
thumbnail images in, 62
uploading pictures using Import button,
    60
web page, 64
iPod
  setting up as external drive, 96
  white, 96
  (see also digital music)
iSight, 40, 77
iSync, 52
iTunes
  "+" button, 73
  encoding music, 72
  Get Info, 74
  importance of using CDDB naming
    service, 71
  launching, 69
  Preferences, 69
  Search window, 75
  Smart Playlists, 74
  (see also digital music)
iTunes Music Store, 67, 68

J
junk mail filter, 35

K

Kensington
    MicroSaver Retractable lock, 98
    Universal Car/Air Adapter, 97
keyboard
    backlighting, xviii
    protector, 7
    special keys, xvii–xx
        function keys (see function keys)
Keyboard & Mouse preference pane, xviii,
    19, 90

L

LaCie's D2 series of external hard drives, 81
LapLogic Chinook T550, 87
LapPad, 87
Lowepro Digital Wallet (D Res 4), 65

M

.Mac accounts and Mail, 35
.Mac mail account, 37
.Mac preference pane, 22
Mail, 34–37
    "+" button, 36
    junk mail filter, 35
    .Mac accounts and, 35
    Preferences, 35

Marware
    Keyboard Cover, 8
    Milano executive case, 5
    SportFolio Sleeve, 4
    WiFi Spy, 93
McDonald's restaurants wireless connec-
    tion, 92
memory, extending, 95
    Crucial Gizmo, 95
    Cruzer Titanium, 95
    iPod, 96
memory card reader, 61
messenger bags, 6
microphone, xv, 22, 39
mini-DVI jack, xv
mirroring, xiii, 18
Monster iTV Link, 82
mouse
    Radtech BT-500, 20
    using, xiv
MP3, 69, 70
music (see digital music)
Music Store, 68, 69, 75

N

Network preference pane, 14, 22, 29, 30
Nokia 6600 phone, 45
number lock toggle button, xviii

O

optical drive, xiii
Option key, xx

P

palmOne Treo, 48
Palm Desktop, 44, 48
PC card expansion slot, xv
Photo Library, 59, 62, 69
    deleting images from, 63
PowerBook
    accessories, 87–99
        extending memory, 95
        travel (see travel accessories)
        USB (see USB accessories)
    sizes, xi
power adapter, configuring, 18
power jack, xiv
Printer List window, 20
Printer Setup Utility, 20
printing, Print & Fax preference pane, 20
Print & Fax preference pane, 20
Protouch iSkin, 7

Q

Quickertek whip antenna, 94
QuickTime preference pane, 23

R

Radtech
    BT-500 mouse, 20
    ScreensavRz protection cloth, 8
Rain Design iLap, 88
Restart, xii
ripping CDs, 68, 71

S

S-Video, xvi
Safari browser, 31–33
    AutoFill icon, 33
    bookmarks, 32
    creating tabs, 32
    Preferences, 32
    scrolling long pages, xix
SanDisk FireWire ImageMate Reader, 61
SanDisk Ultra II memory cards, 65
screen brightness, controlling, xvii
screen protection, 8
Screen Saver button, 14
Security preference pane, 17
security slot, xvi
Sennheiser PX 100 headphones, 72
Sharing preference pane, 24
Shut Down, xii
Sleep mode, xii
slideshows, 64
Smart Playlists, 74
Software Update preference pane, 26
Sony SRS-T88 powered speakers, 68
sound, muting, xvii
Sound Effects preference pane, 21
Sound preference pane, 21
spanning, xiii
Speech preference pane, 27
speech recognition, 27
Spire's Endo messenger bag, 6
Startup Disk preference pane, 27
stereo mini jacks, xv

Stickies, 53–55
STM backpack, 3
streaming music, 75
SuperDrive, xiii
Swiss Memory USB device, 50
System Preferences, 13–29
    .Mac, 22
    Accounts (see Accounts preference
        pane)
    Appearance, 14
    CDs & DVDs preference pane, 18
    Date & Time, 26
    Desktop & Screensaver, 14
    Displays, 18
    Dock (see Dock preference pane)
    Energy Saver, 18
    Energy Saver preference pane
        Schedule and Options panes, 19
    Exposé, 16
    International, 17
    Keyboard & Mouse (see Keyboard &
        Mouse preference pane)
    Network (see Network preference pane)
    opening, xviii
    Print & Fax, 20
    QuickTime, 23
    Security, 17
    Sharing, 24
    Software Update, 26
    Sound, 21
    Speech, 27
    Startup Disk, 27
    tips, 28
    Universal Access, 27

T

ThinkGeek.com, 50
thumbnail images in iPhoto, 62
trackpad, xiv
    tapping, 20
travel accessories, 97
    Kensington MicroSaver Retractable
        lock, 98
    Kensington Universal Car/Air Adapter, 97

U

Universal Access preference pane, 27
USB 2.0 Microhub, 91
USB 2.0 ports, xiv
USB accessories, 89–91
    Griffin Technology PowerMate USB
        multimedia controller and input
        device, 89
    Iogear USB 2.0 Microhub, 91
    Zip-Linq Road Warrior kit, 90
USB printer, setting up, 21

V

video editing (see iMovie)
video mirroring toggle button, xviii
video signal, sending to external monitor,
    xiii
volume
    adjusting in Sound preference pane, 22
    control, xvii

W

webcam, 40, 77
web sites
    Belkin, 61
    creating custom album, 73
    Crucial Gizmo, 95
    Exposé, 17
    Griffin Technology, 89
    iChat, 39
    iKlear Cleaning kit, 9
    iPhoto, 64
    LapLogic, 87
    Marware, 4
    McDonald's restaurants wireless
        connection, 92
    Monster iTV Link, 82
    Nokia, 45
    Quickertek whip antenna, 94
    Radtech, 8
    Rain Design iLap, 88
    SanDisk, 65
    SanDisk Cruzer Titanium, 95
    Sennheiser, 72
    Sony, 68
    Spire, 6
    STM backpacks, 3
    ThinkGeek.com, 50
    Zip-Linq Road Warrior kit, 90
wireless accessories, 92–94
    AirPort Express Base Station, 92
    Marware WiFi Spy, 93
    Quickertek whip antenna, 94

Z

Zip-Linq Road Warrior kit, 90

PowerBook
Fan Book